THE INDIAN WARS

CHRONICLE OF AMERICA'S WARS

Carol H. Behrman

✒ LERNER PUBLICATIONS COMPANY

MINNEAPOLIS

CHAPTER PHOTO CAPTIONS

Introduction: The grim battle site of Wounded Knee in January 1891. At least 150 Lakota Indians, including women and children, died during the fighting with U.S. Cavalry troops on December 29, 1890. An estimated 25 cavalry members were killed that day.

Chapter 1: In this painting, explorer John Cabot claims what is now eastern Canada for King Henry VII of England in 1497. More European explorers followed, claiming lands in North America for their nations. With the arrival of settlers, clashes of culture and land rights between Europeans and Native Americans quickly developed.

Chapter 2: French fur traders paddle canoes through waters in North America. The French and Native Americans established a profitable trade in beaver pelts. The trade, however, often left Native peoples dependent on the fur trade for survival.

Chapter 3: A wampum belt made by members of the Iroquois Confederacy. Each symbol on the belt of beads represents one of the league member groups.

Chapter 4: Settlers arrive in the Northwest Territory in 1788, believing it their right to seize Indian lands. Native American pleas to the U.S. government for help went ignored.

Chapter 5: This Robert Lindneux painting memorializes the Cherokee people's forced removal and migration from their native lands by the U.S. government. More than 4,000 Cherokees died on the journey, called the Trail of Tears, from the southern United States to the Oklahoma Territory between May 1838 and September 1839.

Chapter 6: Settlers move west across the Great Plains in the 1800s. Millions of U.S. settlers pushed into the American West, claiming the remaining Indian lands.

Chapter 7: Many Great Plains Indians built homes called tepees. Tepees could be set up and torn down quickly as the Native Americans followed seasonal buffalo migrations.

Epilogue: A U.S. government agent delivers food rations to a group of Sioux Indians.

Copyright © 2005 by Carol H. Behrman

Lerner Publications Company
A division of Lerner Publishing Group
241 First Avenue North
Minneapolis, MN 55401

Website address: www.lernerbooks.com

To Edward, with thanks for always being there to share his extensive knowledge of history and, even more important, his love

A Note about Geographical References
For clarity and simplicity of geographical referencing, events and locations in this book are often referenced with present-day U.S. region, state, and city names, even though these regions, states, and cities may not have historically been named or existed as such during the time periods described. Where greater clarity is necessary, the description *present-day* accompanies region, state, and city names.

Library of Congress Cataloging-in-Publication Data

Behrman, Carol H.
  The Indian wars / by Carol H. Behrman.
    p.   cm. — (Chronicle of America's wars)
  Summary: Examines the battles and treaties between native peoples and early European settlers of what was to become the United States, from the early 1600s to the late 1800s.
  Includes bibliographical references and index.
  ISBN: 0-8225-0847-8 (lib. bdg. : alk. paper)
  1. Indians of North America—Wars—Juvenile literature. [1. Indians of North America—Wars.] I. Title. II. Series.
E81.B44 2005
973.04'97—dc22   2003016541

Manufactured in the United States of America
1 2 3 4 5 6 – JR – 10 09 08 07 06 05

TABLE OF CONTENTS

INTRODUCTION

Big Foot was a leader of the Miniconjous, a band (small group) of Lakota Sioux Indians. In late December 1890, U.S. soldiers were searching for Big Foot and his people along the Cheyenne River in present-day South Dakota. The U.S. government feared that Big Foot's band was planning to join other Lakotas to stage a violent uprising against white settlers in the area. Already, several bands of Lakotas had gathered at a site called the Stronghold. Their leaders, Short Bull and Kicking Bear, had called for a war to destroy all white people.

But Big Foot and his people were on a mission of peace. They were traveling to meet Red Cloud, another Lakota chief. In the past, Red Cloud had urged the Indians of the area to cooperate with the U.S. government. Big Foot and Red Cloud hoped to convince Short Bull and Kicking Bear to give up their plans for war.

Big Foot's band numbered about 350 men, women, and children. During the journey, Big Foot became sick. Deathly ill with pneumonia, he lay in a wagon coughing up blood. On December 28, U.S. cavalrymen (soldiers on horseback) caught up with Big Foot's band at Porcupine Creek. The Indians put up a white flag of surrender. The soldiers marched the Miniconjous about five miles west to Wounded Knee Creek and ordered them to set up camp for the night. Fearing an Indian attack, the soldiers aimed four Hotchkiss guns—

powerful, rapid-firing cannons—at the Indian camp.

In the morning, Colonel James W. Forsyth of the U.S. Cavalry ordered the Miniconjou men to gather in a clearing. They were told to give up all their weapons. As the soldiers were disarming the Indians, a shot from an Indian rifle suddenly rang out. The scene erupted into chaos.

The soldiers fired on the Miniconjous. The Indian warriors tried to fight back, but they were greatly outnumbered. As Miniconjou women, children, and old men tried to run away, the soldiers cut them down with fire from the Hotchkiss guns. "They shot us like buffalo," one Indian woman recalled.

When the shooting finally ended, dozens of Miniconjous lay dead. The exact number of Indians killed is unknown, but estimates range from 153 to 300. Among the dead was Big Foot. The soldiers herded the surviving Indians into wagons and carried them away. A fierce blizzard began to blow, covering the bodies of the dead.

For more than 300 years, the Native American peoples of North America (American Indians) had been fighting to preserve their land and way of life. They had fought—and lost—many wars against white troops. They had signed treaties (agreements) with the U.S. government, offering to give up or sell some of their land in exchange for peace. But the U.S. government broke most of the treaties, leading to anger, resentment—and war. Although more battles were fought after 1890, historians say that the massacre at Wounded Knee Creek marked the real end of the Indian struggle.

Black Elk was a survivor of the massacre at Wounded Knee Creek. He later said, "When I look back . . . I can still see the butchered women and children lying heaped and scattered all along the crooked gulch. . . . And I can see that something else died there in the bloody mud and was buried in the blizzard. A people's dream died there."

THE COLONIAL WARS

1

In 1492 a Spanish navigator named Christopher Columbus set sail on a dangerous journey across the Atlantic Ocean. Sailing from Spain, he made landings on the Caribbean islands of Cuba and Hispaniola. When Columbus returned to Spain, he claimed to have discovered a "New World." News of Columbus's journey spread throughout Europe. The Age of Discovery had begun.

During the following decades, Columbus and many other explorers made voyages to the so-called New World—Central, South, and North America. Some looked for adventure and the thrill of discovery. Others sought wealth and power. Many explorers claimed portions of America—

and its riches—for their governments in Europe.

In Central and South America, most of the European explorers came from Spain. In North America, where the U.S. Indian Wars were fought, the explorers came from a variety of nations. John Cabot sailed from England in 1497, reaching the coast of present-day Canada. English explorer Sir Walter Raleigh explored the Atlantic coast from North Carolina south to Florida. Spaniard Juan Ponce de León visited Florida in the early 1500s and claimed it for Spain. In 1519 another Spanish sailor, Hernán Cortés, conquered Mexico. Frenchman Jacques Cartier explored the Saint Lawrence River in Canada in the mid-1500s. Frenchman Samuel de Champlain founded the city of Quebec in the early 1600s.

The early European expeditions to North America were soon followed by waves of settlers. They came to make their homes in the fertile, unknown land. Many came to escape the poverty of their homelands. Others came because their rulers at home disapproved of their religious beliefs. These settlers hoped to find better opportunities in the New World, which they saw as a vast, empty land, waiting to be settled.

But the New World was not new to Native Americans. Nor was it empty. Indian peoples had lived in North, Central, and South America for centuries, in different groups, scattered throughout the hemisphere. Each group of peoples had its own unique history, culture, and way of life. Groups sometimes warred with one another and often made alliances. No one knows for certain how many Native Americans once occupied the territory that would later become the United States. Estimates range from one million to more than ten million.

While the Indian peoples of America were very different from one another, they were even more different from the white settlers who started to arrive in their homelands in the 1500s and 1600s. In North America, many Indian peoples did not live in permanent towns. They lived in bands or tribes (bands joined together form tribes), ranging in size from a few dozen (band) to several hundred people (tribe). They hunted wild game and fished from rivers, lakes, and seas. They gathered wild plants and grew crops to feed themselves. Indians didn't claim to own the land they lived on. They tended the land and and generally used its resources carefully.

Native Americans from the Virginia region of North America fish in the 1500s. Like all human cultures past and present, Native Americans developed technology to survive in their environments. The fencing in the painting (above left), for example, confines fish to a limited area, making them easier to catch.

Native American Profile: The Algonquian

Algonquian Indians are a group of nations united by a similar language. The Algonquian homeland stretches along the eastern coast of North America, from the Carolinas north to Canada. Algonquian nations include the Algonquians, Delawares, Kickapoos, Miamis, Mohegans, Mahicans, Narragansets, Ojibwas, Pequots, Potawatomis, Shawnees, and Wampanoags.

The nations share many stories and rituals. For instance, all Algonquian people think of themselves as the original people of the earth because their homelands are in the East, where the sun rises.

Historically, the Algonquians lived mainly in woodlands. They caught fish and hunted deer. They grew corn, beans, and squash. Some nations moved with the seasons. Others stayed in one place all year long. Families lived in dome-shaped houses called wigwams, built with arched poles covered by animal hides, tree bark, or mats of reeds. Northern Algonquians sometimes lived in longhouses during winter. These were sturdy buildings about 100 feet long, shared by several families. Each family had its own living compartment and hearth (fire pit) inside the house. People slept on raised wooden platforms.

Men and women had different tasks. Men cleared the fields, hunted, and fished. They fought to protect their communities during wars. Algonquian women grew crops and did housework. Algonquians were kind to their children and seldom punished them. Children were taught that bad behavior would bring shame on all their people.

Many Algonquian traditions live on in modern life. Algonquian ceremonies and rituals mark the seasons of the year and the stages of life, such as a young person's coming of age (entrance into adulthood) and marriage. The Algonquians also celebrate a baby's first step and first tooth.

Algonquian homes, or wigwams. Like all societies, the Algonquians built homes suited to the environment and to their lifestyles.

White settlers, on the other hand, wanted to create farms, businesses, and cities in North America. They wanted to own land, construct houses and other buildings, and settle in one place. They hoped to grow food on their farms and sell any leftover crops.

Neither the Indians nor the settlers understood the other's culture. And both groups wanted the same land. Misunderstandings and anger grew on both sides. The two peoples could not live peacefully together in North America. War was inevitable.

THE JAMESTOWN COLONY

In 1606 a group of English businessmen created the Virginia Company. Its purpose was to establish English colonies (settlements with ties to England) in the New World. The company was named for Queen Elizabeth I of England—called the Virgin Queen—who had died three years earlier.

In December the Virginia Company sent three small sailing ships, *Susan Constant, Godspeed,* and *Discovery,* to North America. On April 26, 1607, the ships arrived off the coast of Virginia. After sailing up a broad river—which they named the James after their king, James I—the group found a spot that could be easily defended. There, the party of more than 100 men and boys built a town, which they called Jamestown.

The Virginia countryside was bountiful when the colonists arrived in spring. But Virginia winters were harsher than the English expected. By the time winter arrived, the colonists had used up their food supplies. One of the men, Captain John Smith, kept up the spirits of the settlers and helped them gather food such as nuts and berries.

During one expedition to look for food, Smith was captured by local Indians. They were members of the Powhatan Confederacy, an alliance of about 30 different tribes. According to Smith's account, the Indians were about to execute him when a young Indian girl flung herself in front of him and begged her people to spare his life. Her name was Pocahontas, and she was the favorite daughter of the Powhatan chief, Wahunsonacock. Pocahontas had visited the English settlers in Jamestown and had grown to like them.

Wahunsonacock spared John Smith's life. The English captain and the Native American chief became friends. The English settlers called the chief by the name of his confederation, Powhatan, while Smith took the Indian name Nantaquoud. Powhatan and his people helped the colonists survive that first winter. John Smith reported gratefully how the Indians brought them "corn [when] it was half ripe to refresh us when we rather expected . . . they would . . . destroy us."

More colonists soon landed at Jamestown. About 900 came between 1607 and 1610, but only 150 survived the harsh winters. They would all have died had it not been for Powhatan's help.

The tie between Powhatan and the colonists became even stronger in 1616, when Pocahontas married an Englishman named John Rolfe. During the same year, Rolfe and other colonists successfully planted the first tobacco crop in Virginia. They exported the tobacco to Europe, and soon it was in great demand.

Farmers planted more and more tobacco, creating large farms on lands once used by Indians. Jamestown became prosperous, and more English people moved there.

MORE ENGLISH, FEWER INDIANS

Chief Powhatan managed to keep the peace with the English for many years. But the arrival of English colonists brought drastic changes to the Powhatan people.

The Tobacco Business

Before the arrival of Europeans, Native Americans had been smoking the leaves and stems of the tobacco plant for thousands of years. Some Indians grew tobacco in small plots. Others gathered wild tobacco. It was smoked as a medicine and in religious ceremonies.

When Christopher Columbus reached the Caribbean islands in 1492, he saw Arawak people smoking tobacco through a tube of leaves. Columbus's crew brought tobacco back to Spain. Its use spread throughout Europe. At first, Europeans smoked tobacco in an attempt to treat ailments such as migraine headaches, asthma, and cancer. Soon, however, Europeans were smoking for pleasure.

John Rolfe was one of the first colonists to plant tobacco in Jamestown. Others followed his example. They sold the tobacco to merchants in Europe, where the demand for tobacco soared. Soon tobacco growing became a thriving business in the American colonies. Many historians believe that without tobacco, the English colonies in North America would have failed.

The Powhatans grew poorer as they watched tobacco planters take over their lands. Worse, many Indians grew sick and died from diseases brought to North America by the settlers. Indians had no immunity, or natural resistance, to these diseases. The worst killer was smallpox, which often spread with terrible speed, destroying entire Indian villages—sometimes leaving almost no one alive to bury the dead.

In 1618 Chief Powhatan died. The Powhatan Confederacy chose Opechancanough, Powhatan's brother, as its new leader. Opechancanough hated the English for taking his people's lands. He planned a military campaign to drive the English settlers away.

In 1622 Opechancanough led his warriors in a surprise attack on Jamestown. On a Friday morning in March, hundreds of Powhatans attacked farms surrounding the town, striking with arrows and tomahawks (light axes). They killed 347 men, women, and children, almost one-third of the colony's population. Some farmers had been warned about the upcoming attack and fled to the town center for safety. Opechancanough was pleased to see the hated English fleeing from Indian land.

The settlers regrouped and fought back. Armed with muskets and other guns, the Jamestown militia (citizen army) attacked Indian villages, killing hundreds of men, women, and children. The colonists waited to raid Powhatan villages until just before the harvest, when they could destroy crops ready to be picked from the fields. In this way, Indian food supplies were wiped out. The Indians were left to freeze and starve

Quebec•

CANADA

Lake Superior

Lake Huron

Lake Michigan

Lake Ontario

Lake Erie

ABENAKIS

Saint Lawrence River

IROQUOIS CONFEDERACY

MOHAWKS

NIPMUCS

WAMPANOAGS

Plymouth

PEQUOTS

King Philip's War

NARRAGANSETS

SUSQUEHANNOCKS

Rappahannock River

York River

James River

Jamestown

POWHATAN

NORTH AMERICA

ATLANTIC OCEAN

Gulf of Mexico

Miles
0   100   200   300

0   100   200   300   400
Kilometers

**The Colonial Wars
1622–1675**

★ Battle site

‒‒‒ Modern country border

‒·‒ Modern state border

• Settlement

through several severe winters. They also continued to die of disease.

Opechancanough continued his raids year after year. Even so, the Virginia colony kept growing larger and more prosperous. By 1644 more than 10,000 settlers were living in Virginia. In April of that year, the old chief gathered his remaining warriors and made one last effort to drive off the English. At first, the new uprising took the settlers by surprise. Nearly 500 were killed. But then the settlers struck back. The Indians did not stand a chance. Although inaccurate and unwieldy, the muskets white settlers used

Another Killer

Native Americans had no immunity to certain diseases, so illnesses that would usually just make a European sick, such as measles, were often fatal to Indians. Diseases brought from Europe killed Indian peoples in great numbers during the years of the Indian wars. From 1616 to 1618, epidemics of disease swept across southern New England, killing up to 75 percent of the coastal Algonquians. In the early 1630s, smallpox killed about half of the Huron and Iroquois peoples.

This Native American drawing shows an Oglala man infected with measles.

With so many people sick and dying, few people were left to farm, hunt, and carry on other work necessary for survival. As more Indians died, their communities began to crumble. Some nations went to war with one another to obtain the needed resources. Others added to their numbers by taking captives from enemy nations. Some bands merged to maintain their numbers.

inflicted more devastating wounds than did the Indians' arrows and hatchets. The white forces also greatly outnumbered the Powhatans. The Powhatans were defeated. Opechancanough, by then old and frail, was taken prisoner and later shot in the back by a guard.

The Powhatans had been 15,000 strong when the English first arrived at Jamestown. By 1644 only 2,000 Powhatans were left, while about 40,000 English colonists lived in the region. Necotowance, the new Powhatan leader, was forced to make peace. In a treaty made with the English, he swore allegiance (loyalty) to the king of England. He also gave up rights to all the land between the James and York rivers in Virginia. The Indians agreed to stay away from English settlements, and the colonists pledged to keep off the small pieces of land left to the Powhatan.

Thirty years of uneasy peace followed, but the Indians of Virginia were divided among themselves. The English took advantage of this conflict between the groups. They enlisted the help of the Occaneechis to defeat the Susquehannocks, who lived along Virginia's upper Rappahannock River. Then, treacherously turning upon their Occaneeci allies, the English attacked them and wiped them out.

THE MASSACHUSETTS COLONY

Far to the north of Virginia, in the area that would become present-day Massachusetts, a boatload of English settlers arrived at Plymouth Harbor in 1620. They were Puritans, members of a religious group that tried to follow a simple, pure way of life. The Puritans had rigid rules about moral behavior and obeying God's commandments. In England the government persecuted Puritans for their religious beliefs. So a group of Puritans decided to leave their country for the New World, to establish a colony where they could worship in freedom. The group called themselves Pilgrims.

On September 16, 1620, 102 Pilgrims set sail from Southampton, England, on a small ship called the *Mayflower*. They planned to go to Virginia, but halfway across the Atlantic, a raging storm drove the ship off course. On November 9, they sighted land. It was not Virginia, but the coast of Massachusetts. They sailed into a bay and found a good harbor, close to fertile land. They named their new home Plymouth, after Plymouth, England, and set to work building houses and a fort for protection.

The first visitor to the Plymouth settlement was an Indian named Samoset. He knew a little English from an earlier meeting with English fishermen and was able to welcome the newcomers in their own language. Samoset's visit was followed by one from Massasoit, the sachem (chief) of the Wampanoag Nation (a political, economic, and military alliance of tribes). He was accompanied by many of his men.

One of these men, Squanto, stayed behind when Massasoit left. Squanto had been kidnapped by English fishermen and had lived in England for several years. He spoke English well. He showed the Pilgrims how to plant corn, hunt, catch fish, and build canoes. During the summer, when a group of settlers visited Massasoit's camp, he gave them corn seed and tobacco. With the help of Native Americans, the Pilgrims had a rich harvest that autumn. They put away stores of food to last through the winter. They also invited their Indian friends to a great feast—the first Thanksgiving.

The English and the Wampanoags signed a treaty, agreeing to live in peace. The two groups also agreed to be military allies. The Wampanoags were happy to have English allies, who could help them in case of war with their longtime enemies, the Narragansets. The treaty favored the English settlers, however. For example, it said the English could punish Indians who broke English laws, but it gave the Indians no power to punish the settlers.

CLASH OF CULTURES

Many more English settlers arrived in Massachusetts and other parts of New England during the next few years. The settlers cleared forests to make room for farms and towns. They built settlements on land that Native Americans had lived on and used for centuries. These colonists did not believe that the land belonged to the Indians. They saw North America as a wilderness available for the taking. Clearing that wilderness, colonists felt, included clearing it of Indians as well. In fact, Europeans viewed the Indians as "savages"—fierce and untamed like the wilderness itself.

Most Indians lived a nomadic lifestyle—they traveled from place to place seasonally, using the land's resources and then moving on. English settlers wanted to mark out pastures, roads, and boundaries. They didn't want Indians crossing onto what they considered private property. "Our first work is expulsion of the savages to gain the free range of the country for increase of Cattle, swine, etc.," said one English governor. "It is infinitely better to have no [Indians] among us, who at best were but thorns in our sides."

Another culture clash involved religion. Most Indian nations practiced animistic religions. They believed that animals, trees, wind, water, dead ancestors, and other natural elements held spiritual power. To the English settlers, who practiced Christianity, this kind of religion seemed like "devil worship." English missionaries, or religious teachers, were determined to convert native peoples to Christianity.

The missionaries claimed that their religion offered great spiritual rewards. Some Indians—by then ravaged by poverty and disease—were open to the new teachings. They agreed to study Christian teachings, the English language, and European ways. In many places in New England, Indians who

> EYEWITNESS QUOTE:
> A CLASH OF CULTURES
>
> **"Our fathers had plenty of deer and skins . . . our coves full of flesh and fowl. But these English have gotten our land, they with scythes cut down the grass, and with axes fell the trees; their cows and horses eat the grass . . . and we shall all be starved."**
>
> —**Miantonomo, a Narraganset chief**

became Christians moved to "praying towns," all-Indian settlements that were tightly regulated by the English. Many other Indians, however, held fast to their traditional beliefs.

KING PHILIP'S WAR

Chief Massasoit died in 1661, and his son Metacomet (called Philip and then King Philip by the English), became chief of the Wampanoags. By then English colonists outnumbered Indians three to one in some parts of New England. With less and less land for hunting and farming, Indians became dependent on trade with Europeans for their survival. They continued to suffer from epidemics of disease. Worse, English settlers sometimes gave Wampanoags liquor, encouraging drunkenness. Once the Indians were drunk, settlers could trick them into selling their land.

The English put increasing pressure on Indians to act and live like Europeans. In 1671 English officials forced Metacomet to sign a treaty, agreeing that his people

Wampum: Changing Uses

Many nations living along the Atlantic coast made beads from shells, then strung the beads into necklaces and belts called wampum. By arranging the beads in certain designs, which carried meanings, Indians were used wampum to keep records. Belts of wampum were also worn as decoration. When Europeans arrived in North America, Indians and white traders began to use wampum as money. A European trader might give Indians kettles, knives, and other items in exchange for wampum. The trader would then pass the wampum on to other tribes in exchange for animal furs.

would follow colonial laws. These laws greatly curtailed Indian freedoms. For instance, English law said the Wampanoags could not hunt or fish on Sunday, the Christian Sabbath. They could not go to their own medicine men, or healers, when they were ill. They had to ask English officials for permission to do ordinary things, such as purchasing horses.

Metacomet hated how the colonists treated his people. He disliked the missionaries who tried to convert Indians to Christianity and the laws that restricted his people's rights. Metacomet watched the English colonies grow and prosper at the expense of his own people.

Other Indians in the region had similar experiences. Canonchet, chief of the Narragansets, had watched English soldiers massacre 600 of his people in a bloody raid. In 1675 he and the warriors who had survived the raid joined with the Wampanoags to wage war against the English. The Abenakis of southeastern Maine joined the fight after English sailors cruelly drowned the baby son of their chief. The Nipmucs of central Massachusetts also agreed to fight the English. The conflict became known as King Philip's War.

The united nations, led by King Philip, led surprise raids upon colonial villages. They attacked using muskets acquired from white traders—far more effective than tomahawks, arrows, and other traditional weapons. At first, the Native Americans seemed victorious. During the summer and fall of 1675, they attacked 90

Trophies of War

Scalping—removing the hair and skin from the top of an enemy's head with a knife or hatchet—was a common practice in Native American warfare. Warriors generally scalped enemies who were wounded or dying. Taking a scalp was a symbolic substitute for taking the enemy alive. Warriors often dried scalps they had taken and displayed them as trophies.

towns and destroyed 12 of them. Settlers fled in terror.

Later, however, the colonists rallied. They called in their militias. They also took advantage of divisions among Native Americans to create alliances with other Indian nations. The Mohawks and Pequots joined the English. Their warriors taught the colonists how to fight in the wilderness: how to avoid ambushes, how to track down fleeing warriors, and how to find Indian villages. The English and their Indian allies had more soldiers and better weapons than the Wampanoags and their allies. King Philip and his men were forced back in battle after battle. Thousands of Wampanoag and Narraganset warriors were killed. Thousands more Indians died from illness or starvation after their villages were destroyed.

King Philip himself was killed in battle. Chief Canonchet of the Narragansets was captured and sentenced to be executed. "I like it well," he said of his sentence. "I shall die before my heart is soft or I have said anything unworthy of myself."

THE FRENCH
2 AND INDIAN WARS

While English colonists were settling New England and Virginia, French explorers were claiming land farther north. In 1608 French explorer Samuel de Champlain founded the colony of Quebec (in present-day Canada) as a fur-trading center. This colony gave the French control of the eastern Saint Lawrence River.

In 1618 Champlain sent another Frenchman, Étienne Brulé, to explore territory west of Quebec. He traveled as far as present-day Michigan and the Great Lakes. Other French travelers followed. But rather than taking over Indian land for farming, the French were interested in trading. They gave the Indians knives, kettles, cloth, and other equip-

ment in exchange for animal furs. Beaver fur, greatly valued in Europe for fashionable clothing, was highly sought after. Many Indians began to devote all their time to trapping instead of hunting and fishing. The trade was lucrative, but it also made Indians reliant on European traders for their survival.

By the 1670s, France controlled the Great Lakes region and the western part of present-day Ohio. They called their American territories New France. French influence extended even farther into the continent in 1682, when explorer René-Robert Cavelier, sieur de (lord of) La Salle led an expedition from Illinois down the Mississippi River to the Gulf of Mexico. He

A Changing Economy

Before European arrival, Native Americans made everything they needed from resources in their environments. They made pots from clay, axes and knives from stone, needles from animal bone, and leather from animal skins. To make sure they always had fire, they kept coals smoldering and carried them from place to place.

White traders introduced manufactured items that made Indian life easier. They brought the Indians brass kettles, which were stronger than clay pots and better for cooking. They brought ready-made iron knives, axes, and arrowheads. They brought cloth and flint and steel (for making fire). The Europeans also traded glass beads, which Indians used to make wampum and decorations.

Gradually, Indians came to rely on ready-made goods. They lost many of the skills that their ancestors had used for generations. No longer able to fashion clay pots or stone arrowheads, Indians relied on white traders to supply their needs. A Cherokee chief named Skiagunsta commented on the way his people were becoming dependent on Europeans. "The Cloaths we wear, we cannot make ourselves," he said. "They are made for us. We use their Ammunition with which we kill deer. We cannot make our Guns. Every necessary Thing in Life we must have from the White People."

Indians barter blankets and other goods with a French trader.

claimed all the land around the river—from the Appalachian Mountains in the east to the Rocky Mountains in the west—for the king of France, Louis XIV. He named the region Louisiana in honor of the king. By this time, France and England were fighting for control of North America and its riches.

CAUGHT IN THE MIDDLE

Indians were caught in the middle of the conflict between France and England. In fact, they did not trust either the French or the English. They had watched anxiously as settlers from both France and England streamed into North America. They had struggled without success to hold on to their ancient lands and traditions. Many native people had converted to Christianity, the religion of the European newcomers. The old ways that had served Indians well for centuries were weakening.

Both European nations tried to acquire Indian allies. In choosing sides, Native Americans attempted to look out for their own interests. The Hurons, for instance, who had grown to depend on the French fur trade, sided with the French. The Mohawks sided with the English against their traditional foes, the Hurons.

Yet some Indians realized their cause was doomed, no matter which side they chose. When English settlers tried to convince the Delaware people to side against the French, one Delaware man replied, "You intend to drive us away and settle this

Miles
0   100   200   300

0   100   200   300   400
Kilometers

N

FORT
LOUISBOURG

Plains of
Abraham

NEW
FRANCE

CANADA

Lake Superior

Quebec

ABENAKIS

MAINE
(part of
MASSACHUSETTS)

Port
Royal

Saint Lawrence River

Montreal

VERMONT

Lake Huron

Lake Michigan

FORT
FRONTENAC

FORT
TICONDEROGA

NEW
HAMPSHIRE

HURONS

Lake Ontario

FORT
WILLIAM
HENRY

Lake
George

Boston

FORT NIAGARA

FORT
OSWEGO

IROQUOIS   CONFEDERACY

MOHAWKS

Schenectady

MASSACHUSETTS

RHODE ISLAND

Lake Erie

NEW
YORK

Deerfield
Massacre

PENNSYLVANIA

DELAWARES

NEW JERSEY

CONNECTICUT

NEW
FRANCE

FORT
DUQUESNE

FORT NECESSITY

APPALACHIAN   MOUNTAINS

MARYLAND

DELAWARE

Ohio River

VIRGINIA

ATLANTIC
OCEAN

Mississippi River

NORTH CAROLINA

SOUTH
CAROLINA

GEORGIA

Gulf of
Mexico

French
and Indian Wars
1690–1763

Battle site

British colonies

Other territory

New France

Colony border

Modern country border

Modern state border

■ Fort

● City

country, or else, why do you come to fight in the land that God has given us?"

KING WILLIAM'S WAR

France and England had long been enemies. Starting in 1689, the two nations took part in a series of wars that lasted 100 years. The first war soon spread to North America, where it was called King William's War, after King William III of England.

Hoping to enlarge New France into a great empire with its center in Quebec, the French and their Indian allies began raiding English settlements close to their territory. One of these was the tiny English settlement of Schenectady, New York. On a bitter, snowy night in February 1690, a heavily armed force of French and Indian fighters launched a surprise attack. While the townspeople slept, their enemies smashed open the unguarded town gates and stormed in. They set fire to the village. Then, as people tried to flee their burning town, the attackers cut them down with knives and tomahawks. Sixty men, women, and children were killed. Twenty-seven others were taken prisoner and marched north through the icy drifts. "No pen can write, and no tongue express," reported one witness, "the cruelties that were committed." Raids on Salmon Falls in New Hampshire and Fort Loyal in Maine followed the one on Schenectady.

The English colonies began to arm and train soldiers to fight back. In April 1691, seven ships commanded by Sir William Phips sailed out of Boston Harbor. Their destination was French-held Port Royal in Acadia (present-day Nova Scotia) off the coast of Canada. The English forces captured Port Royal, and within a month, all of Acadia surrendered.

Later that year, Phips led an attack into the heart of New France. His force laid siege to (surrounded) Quebec. Phips hoped that blockading the city and cutting off its supply of food and ammunition would force the French to surrender. But the French refused to give in. Months passed, winter set in, and many English soldiers fell ill. When they tried to wade from their ships through the freezing water to shore, the French gunned them down from heights above. Phips and his crippled fleet were forced to return to Boston.

Captain Benjamin Church had better luck the following year. He led 300 soldiers in a series of attacks against one of France's Indian allies, the Abenakis. The soldiers pushed the Indians inland and pursued them relentlessly. Finally, in November, several Abenaki sachems agreed to a truce.

Raids on both sides continued. William Phips built forts along the Massachusetts border, but he could not protect all the small, outlying settlements there. In March 1697, a group of Abenakis attacked the small town of Haverhill, north of Boston. The village was completely unprepared for the violent dawn raid. The Indians killed 27 people, set much of the settlement on fire, and carried off 13 prisoners.

In 1697 England and France signed the Treaty of Ryswick, which ended the fighting in Europe. It also ended King William's War. As part of the agreement, all colonial lands, including Acadia, were given back to the original French or English colonizers. No lands were returned to the Indians.

HARDWARE AND ARMAMENTS

The Indian Wars took place over a period of almost 300 years. Weapons changed during this time. As a rule, weapons used by colonial and U.S. troops were more powerful and plentiful than those used by Native Americans, giving white armies a significant advantage.

Colonial and U.S. Weapons Before the American Revolution, colonial and British troops carried firearms such as muskets and pistols. To load his weapon, a soldier poured gunpowder into the barrel of his gun. He added a cloth wad and a lead ball and pushed them down the barrel with a ramrod. Then the musket or pistol was ready to be fired. Soldiers often attached sharp blades called bayonets to their muskets for use in hand-to-hand combat. Cavalrymen carried carbines, which were shorter than muskets and easier to handle on horseback.

During the 1800s, firearms were greatly improved with the invention of repeating rifles and revolvers, guns that did not require reloading between shots. In the final years of the Indian Wars, army units often took cannons into battle. Their firepower was greater than any other weapon of the time.

Native American Weapons During the early years of the Indian Wars, Native Americans relied on traditional weapons of war such as bows and arrows and tomahawks. These tools were used for both hunting and battle. They were simple but deadly. Indian warriors were trained to use them effectively.

Warriors usually made their own weapons. They made sturdy bows, as tall as a man, from hardwood. The bows had thick handles for easy gripping. Arrows were made by scraping the bark from thin strips of wood. Plains Indians cut grooves along the shafts of their arrows and fastened eagle or turkey feathers to the ends. The grooves and feathers helped keep arrows straight in flight. Early arrowheads were made of sharpened pieces of flint, obsidian (volcanic glass), or bone. Sometimes warriors added poison to arrows to make them deadlier.

A tomahawk was a small axe, with a bone, stone, or metal blade attached to a wooden or metal handle. Warriors used tomahawks like clubs or threw them at enemies. Warriors also went to battle armed with clubs and knives, both used to strike enemies in hand-to-hand combat.

After European arrival, Indians added iron blades to tomahawks and brass tips to arrows. The metal cutting edges were sharper and deadlier than stone or bone edges. Even the greatest warrior, however, was at a disadvantage against the better-armed white soldiers.

White traders gave guns to Indians early in the 1600s, but Indians, at first, continued to rely on their traditional weapons. As time went on, Indians realized the advantages of firearms over traditional weapons. They began to obtain as many rifles and pistols as they could through purchase, trade, or theft. By the 1800s, they were using firearms more regularly in battle.

QUEEN ANNE'S WAR

King William died in 1702. That year a new war broke out between France and England. Once again, the conflict spread to America, where it was called Queen Anne's War, after the new ruler of England.

By then, Philippe de Rigaud de Vaudreuil was the governor in French North America. He persuaded the Abenakis to join the French in a new series of raids on settlements in New England. One of these occurred in February 1704, at the small village of Deerfield in Massachusetts. A force of about 50 Frenchmen and 200 Abenakis silently crept over the town fence during the night, killed 53 settlers, and took 111 others prisoner.

English settlers were outraged. They fought back alongside their own Indian allies, the Mohawks, striking French settlements in small raids. Violent battles raged for several years.

Eventually, the British needed more troops and equipment from their home country (in 1707, Scotland joined England and Wales, forming Great Britain). So in 1709, British commander Francis Nicholson sailed to Britain. To demonstrate the "exotic" wonders of the New World to Queen Anne, he took along four Mohawks, dressed in brightly colored traditional Mohawk clothing. People came from all parts of the city to gaze at the Indians as though they were museum exhibits, not people. The queen was also amazed and impressed by their appearance. She agreed to send five warships, staffed by 400 marines, to America. Led by Nicholson, the British fleet sailed to Port Royal in Acadia, again in the hands of the French. Nicholson succeeded in taking Port Royal once more.

In Europe, the fighting between Britain and France ended with the Peace of Utrecht in 1713. As part of the treaty, France had to give up some of its American territory, including Newfoundland, Acadia, and the Hudson Bay region of northeastern Canada. Britain also gained rights to some of the French fur trade. Despite the treaty, fighting continued between French and British colonists, with Indian bands

After the end of Queen Anne's War, Native American tribes who had sided with the French signed this treaty with Great Britain on July 13, 1713. In doing so, Native Americans promised peace with the British, and concessions of land ownership, trade, and submission to British laws.

joining with the French and the British as well as with each other.

THE FRENCH AND INDIAN WAR

The French and Indian War (1754–1763) was the final conflict between Britain and France for control of northeastern North America. It was long and bloody. This war began in the colonies and boiled over into the Seven Years' War (1756–1763) in Europe. Again, both the French and the British enlisted Indian allies to help them.

In 1748 a group of Virginia-based Englishmen had formed the Ohio Company. This company wanted to settle lands around the upper Ohio River in present-day Pennsylvania. The French also wanted this land. Both the British and the French ignored the fact that this area already belonged to an alliance of Indian nations called the Iroquois Confederacy.

The struggle began with each side building forts in the Ohio River valley. A young major named George Washington led part of the British forces. In 1754 his men suffered defeat at a stockade called Fort Necessity in southwestern Pennsylvania. A year later, the French and British clashed again at Fort Duquesne in present-day Pittsburgh. This time, the French persuaded their Indian allies to join them in battle. As was customary for European armies, the British marched toward the battlefield in organized rows. This approach made them easy prey for French and Indian troops, who attacked from behind trees, rocks, and hills—a style of fighting commonly used by Indians. The British soldiers were confused by the enemy's tactics and

Native American Profile: The Iroquois

The Iroquois were originally a confederacy of Indian nations—the Mohawks, Onondagas, Cayugas, Oneidas, and Senecas—based in New York State. In the 1700s, the Tuscaroras, moving north from the Carolinas, joined the confederacy as well. Each nation sent chiefs to a council, which made important decisions on behalf of the entire confederation.

The region's great forests provided wood for homes and canoes. Iroquois men hunted deer, bears, beavers, rabbits, and muskrats. Sometimes women hunted too. People used every part of a killed animal. They ate its meat, used its hide to make leather, and worked its bones and teeth into tools.

A tribe mark, or symbol, representing the five Iroquois nations in the 1600s

Corn was traditionally the main crop of the Iroquois. They also grew pumpkins, beans, and tobacco. They gathered berries and nuts and boiled sweet syrup from maple sap. They made pottery out of clay and baskets from plant fibers.

Iroquois villages consisted of groups of longhouses. Between 16 and 20 families lived in each longhouse. Each family had its own living compartment. The center of the longhouse was used for community activities.

Battle Tactics

European and Native American soldiers used very different tactics in battle. European armies were very regimented. Troops marched into battle in rows, often approaching the enemy on a wide-open field of battle in broad daylight. They didn't fire their weapons until a commander gave the order to shoot. They stayed in formation as they fought, out in the open, without seeking cover from enemy fire. "Instead of stealing upon each other, and taking every advantage to kill the enemy and save their own people," remarked the Sauk warrior Black Hawk, "they march out in open daylight, and fight, regardless of the number of warriors they may lose!"

Indians, on the other hand, had no organized battle formations. Each warrior fought on his own, without taking orders from a commander. The Indians were expert at hit-and-run tactics. They made quick ambushes and then escaped into the wilderness. They sometimes attacked under cover of darkness. They used the landscape to their advantage, firing at enemies from behind trees, rocks, and hills. The Indians also knew the land better than their white enemies. They hid and moved through familiar territory with ease, while white troops often struggled and got lost.

Sometimes Indians' battle tactics gave them the advantage in combat. Overall, however, the Europeans had the advantage. They had standing armies, made up of professional soldiers whose only job was to fight. Indians had no standing armies. Their warriors were ordinary men who also needed to hunt, farm, and take care of their homes. If they spent too much time fighting, their families and villages suffered. And while the number of Indians (and number of warriors) in North America kept dwindling, new Europeans were constantly streaming into North America in search of opportunities. Many of them signed up to be soldiers.

The Europeans also had more and better weapons than their Indian enemies. By the late 1600s, Indians were fighting with European-made muskets and other firearms, in addition to their traditional hatchets, arrows, and war clubs. But Indians had to obtain firearms from European allies or traders, who cut off their supplies when Native Americans were seen as a threat. When they couldn't get firearms by trade or sale, Indians often resorted to stealing them.

could not defend themselves effectively. When the fighting was over, more than 900 British troops lay dead upon the field. The British commander, General Edward Braddock died two days later of wounds received in battle.

The British had better luck in the north. In September 1755, the British and their Mohawk allies defeated the French and their Caughnawaga allies at Lake George in present-day New York State. The following year, a new French commander, Louis-Joseph de Montcalm-Gozon, arrived in America. His forces captured a British fort at Oswego in northern New York and fought again at Lake George, this time

British troops stand in orderly battle lines on the Plains of Abraham outside Quebec ready to engage French forces there in 1759. The key battle of the French and Indian War went to the British. France lost much of its North American territory, and some Native American groups lost their French ally.

taking the newly built Fort William Henry from the British. Montcalm seemed unbeatable. A group of Native American leaders visited him in Montreal, Canada. "We wanted to see this famous man," one of the chiefs remarked, "who tramples the English under his feet."

In 1756 William Pitt became the British secretary of state. He was determined to conquer the French in North America. Pitt sent thousands of British troops to help in this attempt. In 1758 British and colonial troops captured the French fortress of Louisbourg in eastern Nova Scotia. A short time later, they took Fort Frontenac on Lake Ontario, Fort Niagara between Lake Ontario and Lake Erie, and Fort Ticonderoga in New York.

In the summer of 1759, the British general James Wolfe launched an attack on

Quebec. General Montcalm, commanding the French forces there, believed that no enemy could conquer the fortified city. Wolfe's troops and gunships (armed boats) camped outside the town. Their first attempts to take Quebec were unsuccessful. In September, however, Wolfe's forces reached the Plains of Abraham, a plateau above the town. There, the French and British armies met in a decisive battle. The British were victorious, but both commanders were killed.

Skirmishes continued between the French, the British, and their Indian allies. But the fall of Quebec marked the end of the French and Indian War. In 1763 France signed the Treaty of Paris, giving much of its North American territories to Britain. Although it kept Louisiana, France had lost much of its American empire.

3 REBELLION AND REVOLUTION

The British had relied on various Indian nations to help fight the French. They had given these nations weapons and other gifts in exchange for their assistance. After the French and Indian War, however, Britain and its American colonists no longer needed Native American allies. Breaking treaties and casting off their alliances, they continued their pattern of gobbling up Indian lands for new farms and settlements.

As white settlers moved west, so did the Indian wars. A large-scale fight broke out in the early 1760s near the western Great Lakes. This region was home to the Hurons, Senecas, Ottawas, Miamis, and other nations. In the spring of 1763, Indians began passing strings of wampum from group to group. The Indian nations exchanged such belts to obtain political and military allies.

Gradually, one chief emerged as a leader. His name was Pontiac, chief of the Ottawas. Pontiac urged his people to "drive off your land those dogs clothed in red [British soldiers] who will do you nothing but harm." He planned to attack the British at Fort Pontchartrain in present-day Detroit, Michigan.

He went to the fort with a group of his people, pretending the visit was friendly. The Indians entertained the soldiers with a ceremonial dance. During the performance, Pontiac and his scouts carefully noted the layout of the stockade.

Treaties Made and Broken

Right from the start of European settlement, groups of colonists and Native Americans signed treaties with one another. With treaties, Europeans and Native Americans exchanged many kinds of property: money, furs, weapons, ammunition, land, and wampum, for example. With some treaties, Indians agreed to obey colonial laws or European rulers. With other treaties, whites and Indians established military alliances, agreeing to help one another in warfare. Some treaties established boundaries between Indian and white territories. Others gave hunting or fishing rights to one group or another. With some treaties, Indians even agreed to move to government-assigned Indian territories or reservations (lands set aside for and governed by Native Americans). All treaties were essentially peace treaties—if both sides followed the terms of the treaties, war could be avoided.

A 1769 treaty between the British and Native Americans, granting the British land for money. The symbols are the Indian leaders' signatures.

Whites made treaties with Indians in a show of fair play and diplomacy. Indians signed the treaties because they saw they were outnumbered and outgunned. Fighting a stronger force would have been suicidal, they knew, so they negotiated.

But the treaties were written by whites, in English, and the deals almost always favored them. Indians were unfamiliar with written documents and legal terms. They usually worked through interpreters, who explained the documents using Native American languages. Whites often pressured (or threatened) Indians into signing deals they didn't understand. Most Indians couldn't write—they often signed their names with an X or a pictograph (a picture). The experience of Red Cloud, a Lakota Sioux, was typical. "In 1868 men came out and brought the papers," he said. "We could not read them, and they did not tell us truly what was in them. . . . When I reached Washington the Great Father [president] explained to me what the treaty was, and showed me that the interpreters had deceived me."

Often, after treaties were signed, Indians realized they had gotten a bad deal. Land treaties were often one-sided. For instance, William Henry Harrison, governor of Indiana Territory and later U.S. president, persuaded Indians to sign a series of treaties that granted southern Indiana, most of Illinois, and parts of Wisconsin and Missouri to the U.S. government—all for an average price of less than two cents per acre.

In the end, whites broke almost all the treaties they made with Indians. Often, whites simply didn't uphold their end of the bargain, failing to make promised payments in exchange for land. Sometimes, settlers ignored treaties, moving onto Indian lands illegally and then defending their new homes by force. Other times, whites forced Indians to renegotiate old treaties, with better terms for the whites.

They planned to return a few days later for another visit. This time, they would carry muskets, knives, and tomahawks hidden under their blankets.

Major Henry Gladwin commanded soldiers at the fort. An unknown informant, perhaps a young Indian woman, warned him about the coming attack. When the Ottawas arrived with their blankets thrown over their shoulders, Gladwin was prepared. Every man in the fort was armed and in position. The Indians, seeing the armed soldiers, left without a shot being fired.

Pontiac changed his plan. His warriors surrounded the fort in a siege that lasted for five months. Meanwhile, Pontiac sent war parties to raid outlying farmhouses. British settlers were the main targets, but as time went on, French settlers, too, became targets of Pontiac's men. Scores of settlers were murdered, but the British still held Fort Pontchartrain.

Pontiac and other Indian leaders attacked more British forts throughout the Great Lakes area. One by one, these forts fell to Pontiac's men. A string of forts in Pennsylvania fell to Pontiac's allies, the Senecas. Fort Pontchartrain held steadfast, but battles continued elsewhere. During the spring and summer of 1763, 2,000 British soldiers and settlers and many hundreds of Native Americans were killed. Gradually, the better-armed British won a series of victories. The Indians were also weakened by disagreements among the nations, as well as by disease and lack of arms.

Some nations made separate treaties with the British. They agreed to return captured forts in exchange for gifts and ammunition. In October Pontiac, too, was forced to ask for peace. His rebellion was over. Two years later, Pontiac was shot in the back and killed by a member of the rival Peoria peoples. As the tribes and nations of the Great Lakes weakened, white settlers rushed in to take their land.

THE AMERICAN REVOLUTION

In the late 1760s and early 1770s, Indians watched as colonists began to quarrel with their king in Britain. The British government taxed the colonists to help pay the costs of the French and Indian War. The American colonists were upset. Unlike citizens in Britain, colonists could not vote or send elected leaders to represent them in the British government. They complained of "taxation without representation."

When the American colonists protested, the king sent more troops to the colonies. These soldiers angered the colonists even more, and battles broke out between British troops and colonial militias. The American Revolution (1775–1783) had begun. The thirteen colonies each sent representatives to Philadelphia, to a meeting called the Continental Congress. In July 1776, the representatives declared the colonies' independence from Britain, forming the United States of America. But the British government had no intention of letting the colonies break free. It sent more soldiers to crush the rebellion.

At first, the Continental Congress asked Native Americans not to take sides in the war. In a written statement, colonial leaders said that the Revolution was "a family quarrel between us and Old England. You Indians are not concerned in it. We don't wish you to take up the hatchet against the king's troops. We desire you to remain at home, and not join either side, but keep the hatchet buried deep."

But soon the colonists changed their minds and asked for Indian help. Ethan Allen of Vermont asked the Iroquois to fight with his militia. "Join with me and my warriors like brothers," he urged, and he promised to give them "money, blankets, tomahawks, knives, and paint." A British colonel, however, warned the Indians not to trust the colonists. He said the colonists intended to "take all your lands from you and destroy your people."

At first, the six Iroquois nations tried to stay neutral, but their confederation soon fell apart. The Oneidas and the Tuscaroras became U.S. allies. The Mohawks, Cayugas, Senecas, and Onondagas sided with the British. Mohawk war chief Thayendanegea, called Joseph Brant by the British, explained their decision. "Every man of us thought that, by fighting for the King, we could ensure for ourselves and our children a good inheritance [compensation, such as land, after a British victory]."

THE BATTLE OF ORISKANY

In the summer of 1777, a British force of 1,700 men surrounded Fort Stanwix in northern New York. This action was part of a British plan to gain control of the Hudson River and prevent U.S. troops and supplies from moving either north or south along the river. Half of the British troops were regulars (soldiers from the main British army). Half were Seneca and Mohawk warriors, led by Joseph Brant. They expected to easily overcome the small U.S. militia at the fort.

Then a warning arrived that a larger U.S. force, headed by General Nicholas Herkimer, was on its way to help Fort Stanwix. The British commander sent Sir John Johnson and Joseph Brant to stop the new U.S. troops from reaching the fort. About 70 British and 400 Indian soldiers waited in a marshy ravine near Oriskany Creek. The U.S. troops marched right into the trap.

The British and Indians opened fire from their hiding places in the woods. Some Indians swung clubs or tomahawks. Others thrust spears and fired guns at the unprepared U.S. forces. One warrior described the bloodshed as "a stream running down on the . . . ground." Five hundred U.S. troops, including General Herkimer, were slaughtered during the Battle of Oriskany.

Mohawk sachem Tiyanoka is shown holding a hatchet, a traditional Native American battle implement, while wearing a British uniform. Native American groups were forced to choose sides during the American war for independence.

Miles

0   100   200   300

0   100   200   300   400

Kilometers

CANADA

Lake Superior

Lake Huron

Lake Michigan

OTTAWAS

ONONDAGAS

CAYUGAS

Lake Ontario

HURONS

FORT
NIAGARA

SENECAS

Genesee River

IROQUOIS

CONFEDERACY

TUSCARORAS

ONEIDAS

MOHAWKS

FORT
STANWIX

**Battle of
Oriskany**

Saint Lawrence River

VERMONT

MAINE
(part of
MASSACHUSETTS)

NEW
HAMPSHIRE

MASSACHUSETTS

NEW YORK

Hudson River

RHODE ISLAND

CONNECTICUT

**Battle of
Minisink**

FORT
PONTCHARTRAIN

Mississippi River

Illinois River

Peoria

MIAMIS

PENNSYLVANIA

Philadelphia

DELAWARES

NEW JERSEY

MARYLAND

DELAWARE

Ohio River

APPALACHIAN MOUNTAINS

VIRGINIA

ATLANTIC
OCEAN

NORTH CAROLINA

CHEROKEES

CHICKASAWS

SOUTH
CAROLINA

Augusta

GEORGIA

CHOCTAWS

CREEKS

Savannah

FLORIDA (SPAIN)

Gulf of Mexico

N

The Revolutionary
War Period
1763–1783

✦   Battle site

British colonies

Other territory

— · — Modern country border

— · · — Modern state border

■   Fort

●   City

MEDICAL CARE

Overall medical care was poor during the Indian wars. Over the centuries, treatments used by white doctors improved, saving more and more wounded soldiers. At the same time, Indian healers relied on traditional remedies, passed down through the generations.

Treating Soldiers In the 1600s and 1700s, doctors could do little to help wounded colonial or British soldiers. They had few treatments for pain and no antibiotics to treat infections. Doctors had not yet learned that germs cause infections, so they did not wash their hands or put on clean clothing before treating patients.

Sometimes doctors had to cut bullets or arrows from the bodies of wounded soldiers. Often they had to amputate (cut off) wounded arms and legs. Such surgery was primitive, performed at makeshift hospitals near the battlefield, with dirty knives and saws. Afterward, wounds often became infected or wouldn't stop bleeding. Wounded soldiers were left on cots until they either got well or died.

Doctors first used laughing gas (nitrous oxide) in the early 1800s. This gas was sometimes effective in easing pain during surgery. Chloroform, another painkiller, was used later in the century. If doctors didn't have painkilling drugs, they gave patients whiskey to reduce the agony of amputation and other surgery.

By the time of the Civil War, in the mid-1800s, surgical skills had improved and doctors knew more about the importance of cleanliness when treating patients. The U.S. Army set up hospitals, where wounded soldiers could receive care. Many, however, still died from infection and disease.

Treating Native American Warriors Medical care among Native Americans was quite different. Indians generally believed that illness and infection were, in part, caused by supernatural powers. Therefore, shamans (medicine men and medicine women) used prayers, rituals, and songs to cast off spirits causing or contributing to sickness. They also tried to rid sick people of evil spirits by drawing blood, or by making the sufferer sweat or vomit.

Shamans of many Indian peoples, including the Shawnees, Kickapoos, and Potawatomis, bundled together herbs, seeds, feathers, stones, or bones that had been gathered in places thought to have spiritual power. Warriors wore these bundles in battle for protection from injury. "We value our medicine bags so highly," said one Sauk warrior, "that we would not part with them while life endures."

Shamans also had a great knowledge of herbal medicine. They often used herbs, roots, and other plant parts to treat wounds and illnesses. They used treatments made from willow bark to relieve pain, from oak bark to cleanse wounds, and from prickly ash bark to treat coughs. Shamans also made splints for broken bones and tourniquets to stop blood flowing from a wound. They used simple surgery to remove bullets and sew up wounds.

Later, other U.S. forces arrived, led by General Benedict Arnold. They helped keep the British from taking Fort Stanwix. But bands of Iroquois warriors loyal to the British roamed the New York countryside, driving off settlers and destroying homes.

THE BATTLE OF MINISINK

On July 22, 1779, Joseph Brant led a raiding party in a series of skirmishes in southeastern New York. The warriors surprised a colonial settlement at Minisink (present-day Port Jervis), leaving behind scalped victims and burning houses. This attack was followed by a deadly battle on the heights above Minisink Ford. A U.S. militia had gathered quickly after the initial attack. They were defeated in bloody combat.

> **EYEWITNESS QUOTE: WASHINGTON'S STRATEGY**
>
> **"Lay waste to all the [Indian] settlements around that the country [Indian land] may not be merely overrun but destroyed."**
>
> **—General George Washington, to his troops**

As more Indian raids took place in the area, George Washington, by then a general in command of the U.S. forces, began a campaign to weaken his Iroquois enemies. He sent an expedition under Major General John Sullivan to the Genessee River in New York and back. Following Washington's order, the U.S. soldiers destroyed every Iroquois village along the way, chopping down orchards and burning cornfields. Thousands of Indians took refuge with the British at Fort Niagara. From there, the Iroquois continued raids against U.S. forces.

WAR IN THE SOUTHEAST

In the South, both Britain and the United States also pressured Indian leaders to join the fight. Forced to choose sides, the Cherokee, Chickasaw, Choctaw, and Creek nations threw their support behind the British. They did not want to help the colonists, who had taken their land. They also feared that a U.S. victory would mean the loss of even more territory.

Caught between the British and rebellious colonists, Mohawk leader Thayendanegea (Joseph Brant) decided it was wisest to ally his people with the powerful British during the American Revolution. The British abandoned Brant and their other Indian allies when the American colonists won the war.

In 1776 the Cherokees began to raid U.S. settlements from Virginia to Georgia. Together with British troops, they attacked a U.S. stockade in North Carolina. Whites were enraged. U.S. troops marched through 50 Cherokee villages, leaving a path of destruction. They burned down houses and destroyed crops the Indians needed to survive the coming winter. When the campaign ended, 2,000 Indians were dead. Their homeland was in ruins. In May of the following year, the Cherokees surrendered.

Creek, Chickasaw, and Chocktaw warriors continued to fight, helping the British in several other battles. In 1780 the Creeks joined British troops in an attack on Augusta, Georgia. The following year, the Creeks aided the British during a siege of Savannah, Georgia. Emistesigo, a Creek chief, died trying to break through U.S. lines.

A NEW NATION

The American Revolution ended with a U.S. victory. U.S. and British negotiators met in Paris in 1783 to draft a peace treaty. The treaty established the borders of the new United States: from the Atlantic Ocean in the East to the Mississippi River in the West; from the Great Lakes in the North to the Florida border in the South.

Indian leaders such as Joseph Brant had hoped that as part of the treaty negotiations, Britain, "for whom we have so freely bled," would look out for its Indian allies and insist that land in the new nation be set aside for Native Americans. But the British abandoned their former allies. Treaties signed with the Americans made no mention of protection of Indian land.

John Dickinson, a Pennsylvania official, summed up the attitude of many U.S. leaders after the war. He declared "that peace has been made with Great Britain . . . that the back country with all the forts is thereby ceded [given] to us; that [the Indians] must now depend upon us for their preservation and, that unless they immediately cease from their outrages . . . we will instantly turn upon them our armies that have conquered the king of Great Britain . . . and extirpate [remove] them from the land where they were born and now live."

More Europeans arrived to make their homes in the new United States. And U.S. citizens kept moving west onto Indian lands. As numbers of white Americans increased, numbers of Native Americans continued to shrink. A Seneca chief named Red Jacket looked sadly toward the future. He said: "We stand a small island in the bottom of the great waters. . . . They rise, they press upon us and the waves will settle over us and we shall disappear forever."

4 WARS IN THE NORTHWEST TERRITORY

In 1787 the new United States of America adopted a constitution. It stated that the country would be a democracy, with white male citizens choosing their own leaders. The constitution gave no rights to women, black slaves, or Native Americans.

War and diseases had by then severely weakened eastern Native American tribes and nations. Some, such as the Cherokee, stayed near their historic lands and tried to live in peace with European Americans. Other Indians moved westward, joining groups that were already there.

White settlers, meanwhile, set out to conquer the American frontier, which at that time started at the Appalachian Mountains. More than 50,000 white Americans moved into what are now Kentucky and Tennessee during and after the war. Tens of thousands more streamed into what would soon be the states of Ohio and Indiana. They settled on Indian land. Indians protested to the new U.S. government, but the government did not respond. U.S. settlers continued to seize Indian land. More fighting took place, this time in the Northwest Territory (present-day Ohio, Indiana, Illinois, Michigan, Wisconsin, and part of Minnesota).

ST. CLAIR'S SHAME

Michikinikwa, called Little Turtle, was a strong and outspoken leader of the Miami people, based in Ohio and Indiana. Determined to protect Indian land from whit settlers, he convinced several nations in the territory to unite. These included the Miami and the Shawnee nations. Their warriors raided white settlements in Ohio, Indiana, and Illinois.

In 1790 George Washington, by then president of the United States, ordered General Josiah Harmar to stop the raids. General Harmar marched into the troubled territory in September with 1,400 troops. But the warriors under Little Turtle's command outwitted Harmar. Instead of facing the soldiers in a direct battle, Little Turtle's men staged short surprise ambushes, then disappeared into the wilderness. They drew Harmar's soldiers deep into the forest. The U.S. troops became disorganized and ran short of supplies. The Indians killed several hundred soldiers, and General Harmar was forced to withdraw.

The following year, President Washington sent another force against Little Turtle. This time General Arthur St. Clair, the governor of the Northwest Territory, commanded the troops. St. Clair was an experienced soldier. He had fought with the British before the American Revolution and then with the Americans under George Washington. But like Harmar, St. Clair did not understand Native American battle tactics.

In October 1791, St. Clair began his march into the Ohio wilderness with 2,300 men. Most of his troops were new and untrained, with only a few experienced soldiers. By the time St. Clair had found a spot to make a stand, 600 of his men had already deserted. The men camped on high ground overlooking the Wabash River in

Indiana. But St. Clair did not build any fortifications or lookout posts there.

Early on the morning of November 4, Little Turtle and 1,000 warriors surrounded the sleeping soldiers. Jolted awake, the soldiers grabbed their guns and tried to defend themselves, but 650 were killed and hundreds more wounded. Only 580 soldiers, including General St. Clair, survived the campaign. Humiliated by his defeat (which was labeled St. Clair's Shame), St. Clair resigned from the army the following year.

THE BATTLE OF FALLEN TIMBERS

President Washington was desperate to find a commander who could defeat Little Turtle. His next choice was General Anthony Wayne. General Wayne, a tough, experienced soldier, respected the bravery and skill of the warriors under Little Turtle's command. He was determined not to make the same mistakes as Harmar and St. Clair.

In 1792 Wayne gathered an army of 200 men. He spent a year training this force for frontier warfare—fighting in the wilderness in the style of Indians. He also recruited 1,000 sharpshooters (expert shots) from Kentucky who had already fought against Indians. Warriors from the Chickasaw and Chocktaw nations, traditional enemies of Little Turtle's confederation, also volunteered to join Wayne.

Little Turtle knew his men did not stand a chance against the larger force Wayne had brought together. He advised the leaders of his confederation to seek peace. "The Americans are now led by a chief who never sleeps," he told the leaders.

Miles
0   100   200

Kilometers
0   100   200   300

Lake Superior

CANADA

OJIBWAS
OTTAWAS

HO-CHUNKS

Lake Huron

Lake Michigan

HURONS
Battle of the Thames

POTAWATOMIS

Battle of Fallen Timbers

Lake Ontario

Lake Erie

Thames River

Maumee River

Tippecanoe River

Battle of Tippecanoe

St. Clair's Shame

Prophet's Town

MIAMIS

OHIO (1803)

Wabash River

Ohio River

SHAWNEES

KENTUCKY (1792)

Mississippi River

TENNESSEE (1796)

CHEROKEES

CHICKASAWS

CHOCTAWS

GEORGIA (1788)

SOUTH CAROLINA (1788)

NORTH CAROLINA (1789)

CREEKS

VERMONT (1791)

NEW HAMPSHIRE (1788)

MASSACHUSETTS (1788)

NEW YORK (1788)

RHODE ISLAND (1790)

CONNECTICUT (1788)

PENNSYLVANIA (1787)

DELAWARES

NEW JERSEY (1787)

MARYLAND (1788)

DELAWARE (1787)

APPALACHIAN MOUNTAINS

VIRGINIA (1788)

ATLANTIC OCEAN

R. Saint Lawrence River

FLORIDA (SPAIN)

Gulf of Mexico

N

Wars in the Northwest Territory 1790–1813

★ Battle site

☐ United States

▨ Louisiana Purchase

▧ Northwest Territory

☐ Other Territory

– ·· – Period border

– · – Modern country border

– · – Modern state border

● City

SOLDIERS, WARRIORS, AND DRESS

The Indian Wars spanned hundreds of years and stretched across the entire North American continent. Therefore, uniforms and battle dress varied, depending on the era, location, army, and native group involved.

Colonial and U.S. Soldiers During the colonial period, British soldiers were called redcoats because they wore scarlet jackets. They also wore white trousers tucked into heavy boots and black felt hats trimmed with lace. Each soldier carried a knapsack containing a blanket, an extra shirt, food, a penknife, and a razor. Many British soldiers in North America were poor laborers or farmers who joined the army for a steady paycheck. British officers were usually career military men from the upper classes. They fought Indians to obtain additional land for the king.

Colonial soldiers were not as well equipped or well dressed as the British. Their uniform usually consisted of a dark blue jacket with a red lining and white or brown breeches (trousers). Because colonial troops didn't have much money, many men didn't receive an official uniform. They went to war wearing their own clothing. Men from all stations of life fought with colonial militias against the Indians. They fought the Indian Wars to obtain land for their new country.

Depending on the year and unit, the U.S. Army uniform varied during the 1800s. By the time of the Civil War, the regulation army uniform was a nine-button blue coat and light blue pants. Most soldiers continued to wear the Civil War–era uniform when fighting Indian Wars in the West, after the Civil War had ended. Others wore frontier gear, such as buckskin jackets and leather leggings.

Native American Warriors The dress of Native American warriors varied by tribe and nation. On the plains, some warriors wore only leather breechcloths (aprons around the waist). Warriors of the northeastern woodlands often dressed in leather shirts and leggings made from deer hide. Most warriors placed feathers in their hair. Some wore huge, feathered battle headdresses. All warriors used similar weapons such as tomahawks, clubs, knives, and later, firearms.

Indian boys trained for many years to become warriors. When it was time for war, tribes and nations often prepared by holding a special war dance.

Also to prepare for war, shamans performed sacred rituals to find out if the spirits were looking kindly upon the campaign. Plains Indians would never attack at night unless the moon was out. Plains warriors did not want to be killed in the dark, lest their spirits wander in darkness forever.

Before setting out, warriors sometimes painted their bodies and faces. They used colors and patterns to frighten their enemies and bring protection from spirits.

Some warriors (mostly Plains Indians) had a system called counting coup to rate their own courage and success. In this system, warriors earned coup by touching an enemy during battle or capturing an enemy's horse or weapons. Warriors with the most coup held places of honor among their people.

"There is something that whispers to me . . . to listen to offers of peace." But the other chiefs of the confederation wanted to keep fighting. So Little Turtle and his 250 Miami warriors left the group. He turned over command to the Shawnee chief, Blue Jacket.

Blue Jacket led his men to Fallen Timbers, a deep ravine on the Maumee River west of Lake Erie. The ground there was littered with trees that had fallen during a storm. The trees offered many hiding places. Blue Jacket hoped to ambush Wayne's forces there. Borrowing an Indian tactic, General Wayne kept them waiting for several days before attacking. While waiting, the Indians became hungry and went off to hunt for food. Then Wayne attacked in full force. Blue Jacket's warriors were overwhelmed and fled. Hundreds were killed. Wayne lost only 33 men.

On August 3, 1795, the defeated Native Americans were forced to sign the Treaty of Greenville. In it they signed away most of their lands in the Northwest Territory, including large portions of Ohio and Indiana. In exchange, the government gave the Indians rights to hunt in certain places, $20,000 worth of goods, and an annual payment of $9,500. The treaty cleared the way for white settlement in the Ohio Valley.

NEW POLICIES

For more than ten years, no further Indian resistance was organized against U.S. expansion. The United States continued to increase in size, adding more states and territories. In 1803 President Thomas Jefferson doubled the size of the country when he purchased the Louisiana Territory from France. This territory included a vast stretch of land between the Mississippi River and the Rocky Mountains.

Before the American Revolution, Jefferson had hoped that Indians would assimilate (be absorbed) into white society. He hoped that Indian men would take up farming and Indian women would tend to the home—much as white Americans did. If Indians would give up hunting, Jefferson believed, then they would stay in one place and respect the idea of private property.

But as the Indian wars dragged on, and whites and Indians continued to misunderstand one another's culture, Jefferson gave up his notions of assimilation. The only solution to the "Indian problem," Jefferson felt, was to keep Indians and whites separated. To that end, he supported moving Indians out of the eastern United States, into the new Louisiana Territory. Starting in the early 1800s, the U.S. government began pressuring Indians to sign treaties that required them not only to give up their land but also to move west of the Mississippi River.

THE BATTLE OF TIPPECANOE

In the Ohio River valley, one warrior refused to cooperate with the U.S. government. Tecumseh, a Shawnee war chief, had stood by Little Turtle's side against Harmar and St. Clair. Later, he fought bravely at Fallen Timbers, where he saw his brother killed. Tecumseh had refused to sign the Greenville peace treaty. "Sell a country?" he said. "Why not sell the air, the great sea, as well as the earth? Did not the Great Spirit [the supreme Indian god] make them all for the use of his children?"

Against the orders of Shawnee war chief Tecumseh, his younger brother, Tenskwatawa, leads a raid on a U.S. Army camp along the banks of the Tippecanoe River in 1811. After two hours of bloody combat, Tenskwatawa's men ran out of ammunition and had to quit the battle.

Following the defeat at Fallen Timbers, Tecumseh tried to convince local nations to again stand as one against the United States. He knew that to sell their land meant sure destruction. "Where today are the Pequot? Where are the Narraganset, the Mohawk, the Pocanet and other powerful tribes of our people?" he asked. "They have vanished before the . . . white man, as snow before the summer sun." Native Americans rallied to Tecumseh's call. He was an imposing figure—more than six feet tall—a learned man, and a spellbinding speaker.

Tecumseh's younger brother, Tenskwatawa, also worked to unite the Indians. Called the Shawnee Prophet, Tenskwatawa preached a return to traditional Indian values and lifestyle. He urged Indians to resist pressure to adopt white customs and religion. He insisted that they resist the temptations of alcohol.

The two brothers gathered their followers in the village of Tippecanoe in the Indiana Territory. The gathering included Shawnee, Ottawa, Huron, Ho-Chunk, Potawatomi, and Ojibwa people. They called their settlement Prophet's Town.

Whites in the Indiana Territory were suspicious of the Indian alliance. Tecumseh's growing influence also alarmed the territory's governor, William Henry Harrison, who feared that large numbers of Native Americans would settle in and around Prophet's Town. In the fall of 1811, Harrison marched 1,000 U.S. soldiers to the settlement. The army camped on Burnet's Creek,

EYEWITNESS QUOTE: ON TECUMSEH

"The words fell in avalanches from his lips. His eyes burned. . . . His voice resounded . . . now sinking in low and musical whispers, now rising to the highest keys, hurling out his words like a succession of thunderbolts."

—A white man, describing a speech by Tecumseh

near the mouth of the Tippecanoe River. Tecumseh was away, speaking to other Indian nations. He had ordered the Shawnee Prophet to avoid battle until he return. But the Shawnee Prophet ignored his brother's advice. He believed that the Great Spirit had granted him magical powers. He assured his warriors that the U.S. soldiers would be helpless in the face of such powers.

Before dawn, the Shawnee Prophet's forces approached the U.S. camp. A guard saw the Indians coming and shot his gun, warning the other soldiers. They awoke to the roar of Indian muskets and the shouts of oncoming warriors.

The U.S. soldiers were inexperienced and confused. A terrible battle raged for more than two hours. The ground was bloodied with the bodies of dead and wounded from both sides. Then, Tenskwatawa's warriors found that they were running out ammunition. They had to leave the battle. Harrison had lost 68 men. No one knows for sure how many Native Americans died that day, but it is estimated that about 50 of Tenskwatawa's warriors fell. There was no decisive victory for either side.

Disappointed in the failure of the Shawnee Prophet's powers, his followers deserted him and abandoned Prophet's Town. The next day, Harrison's forces marched in and burned the settlement to the ground. The alliance that Tecumseh had formed split apart. The great chief was not beaten, however. He stood in the ashes of Prophet's Town and swore revenge upon U.S. forces.

THE BATTLE OF THE THAMES

With his own Shawnee warriors, Tecumseh continued to raid U.S. settlements. The United States went to war with Great Britain in the War of 1812 (1812–1815), over disagreements about maritime (ocean) shipping, treatment of sailors, and trade. Reviving the old British-Indian alliance against the United States, Tecumseh's forces joined with the British during this war.

Together, Tecumseh and the British fought successful campaigns against U.S. forces around the Great Lakes, taking several U.S. forts. Other Native Americans joined Tecumseh, until soon he was leading a force of 2,000 warriors from 30 different tribes and nations. The British showed their appreciation for Tecumseh's help by giving him the high rank of brigadier general in their army.

British successes ended when a new British commander, General Henry Proctor, replaced Major General Isaac Brock, who had been killed in battle. In the spring of 1813, Proctor retreated from U.S. forces near Lake Erie. William Henry Harrison, by then a general in the U.S. Army, pursued the enemy. On October 5, Tecumseh convinced General Proctor to make a stand on the Thames River in Ontario, Canada. When the 3,500-man U.S. force attacked, Proctor's troops fled deeper into Canada. But Tecumseh and his warriors fought on. The chief reportedly stood his ground, taking shot after shot until he died of a gunshot wound to the chest.

5 INDIAN REMOVAL

Tecumseh had spread his message of unity to many Indian nations, including the Creeks of Georgia and Alabama. In 1811 Tecumseh had spoken at their yearly tribal council. Many of those who heard him were moved by his words. They believed that to survive, Native Americans had to return to traditional ways and that they could do so only by defeating whites in war. Other Creeks opposed war. They feared that the U.S. government and its army were too powerful to be defeated.

By 1813 the Creeks had divided into two groups—one for peace and the other for war. Those who favored war united behind a chief named Red Eagle and began to attack white settlers. They became known as the Red Sticks, because they carried war clubs painted red.

Red Eagle and his warriors attacked at an outpost called Fort Mims, located on the Alabama River. Five hundred settlers, protected by a small group of soldiers, had taken refuge from Indian raiders there. On the afternoon of August 30, 1813, Red Eagle and his war party stormed through the open gates of the fort. The U.S. troops fought for hours against Red Eagle's larger force. The Creeks shot burning arrows into buildings, setting the complex ablaze. The terrified residents ran outside, fleeing the flames. Thirty-six of them were able to escape to safety. The rest were killed by Red Eagle's men.

CANADA

Lake Superior

Mississippi River

HO-CHUNKS

WISCONSIN
(1848)

MINNESOTA
(1858)

Lake Michigan

Lake Huron

MICHIGAN
(1837)

Lake Ontario

Saint Lawrence River

MAINE
(1820)

VERMONT

NEW
HAMPSHIRE

MASSACHUSETTS

SIOUX

*Stillman's
Run*

**Black
Hawk War**

SAUKS

FOX

IOWA
(1846)

● Saukenauk

ILLINOIS
(1818)

INDIANA
(1816)

OHIO

Lake Erie

NEW
YORK

PENNSYLVANIA

RHODE
ISLAND

CONNECTICUT

NEW JERSEY

DELAWARE

Ohio River

MISSOURI
(1821)

Cherokee Trail of Tears

KENTUCKY

APPALACHIAN MOUNTAINS

VIRGINIA

MARYLAND

INDIAN
TERRITORY
(1825)

TENNESSEE

CHEROKEES

NORTH CAROLINA

ARKANSAS
(1836)

Mississippi River

New Echota ●

ALABAMA
(1819)

*Tallapoosa
River*

SOUTH
CAROLINA

TEXAS
(1845)

MISSISSIPPI
(1817)

**Battle of
Horseshoe
Bend**

Alabama River

CREEKS

GEORGIA

LOUISIANA
(1812)

■ **FORT MIMS**

● Pensacola

SEMINOLES

**Second
Seminole War**

**First
Seminole
War**

FLORIDA
(1845)

**Third
Seminole War**

Gulf of Mexico

EVERGLADES

*ATLANTIC
OCEAN*

Seminole Wars
and Indian Removal
1813–1858

✦ Battle site

☐ United States

▨ Other territory

–∙∙–∙∙– Country border

–∙–∙–∙– Modern country border

–∙–∙–∙– State border

–∙–∙–∙– Modern state border

■ Fort

● City

Miles

0   100   200   300

0   100   200   300   400

Kilometers

On the march to engage the Creek Red Sticks in 1814, General Andrew Jackson threatened to shoot anyone in his Tennessee militia who attempted to desert.

THE BATTLE OF HORSESHOE BEND

The killings at Fort Mims were reported in newspapers throughout the country. U.S. citizens called for revenge. Immediately following the event, Tennessee's government approved $300,000 to train an army to fight the Red Sticks. General Andrew Jackson was put in command. The Creeks feared and respected Jackson, a well-known Indian fighter. Within nine days of receiving his assignment, he had assembled 3,500 soldiers. He led them south to Alabama at a rapid pace. A force of Cherokees, Choctaws, and pro-U.S. Creeks joined them.

The Tennessee troops marched deep into Creek country. They pursued the Red Sticks for nearly four months through Georgia and Alabama, defeating them in skirmishes at Tallushatchee and Talladega. Jackson's men were hungry and tired after months of marching and fighting. Some wanted to go home. But Jackson knew the key to defeating the Red Sticks was to beat them in one large battle. He threatened to shoot the first soldier who tried to desert. Not one man left.

In March 1814, Jackson's men continued on to Horseshoe Bend on the Tallapoosa River in Alabama. Nine hundred Red Sticks were waiting behind a huge log barrier. Jackson's men, 2,000 strong, crossed the log barricade. Hours of heavy fighting followed. By nightfall more than 800 Creek warriors lay dead.

In less than a year of fighting, about 3,000 Native Americans lost their lives in the Creek War. Andrew Jackson then forced Creek leaders to sign a treaty, giving up 23 million acres of territory—half of their land. Most Creeks gave up their dreams of independence at that point and lived on peacefully for the time being, in the small settlements that were left to them. But some young Creek warriors fled south to Florida, joining a group called the Seminoles. There, they continued their fight for freedom.

THE SEMINOLE WARS

The Seminoles, relatives of the Creeks, had originally lived in Georgia and Alabama. European settlers had forced them off their lands in the early 1700s. They fled south to Florida, which was then owned by Spain. The Seminoles sympathized with another oppressed group in the United States, African American slaves. In the early 1800s, many slaves escaped from plantations in the American South and took refuge among the Seminoles. The Seminoles welcomed them, sharing their land and sometimes marrying African Americans.

Enraged, slave owners in the United States sent troops across the Florida border to bring back runaway slaves. The Seminoles and their African American friends fought back side by side. In 1817 Andrew Jackson led 3,000 U.S. troops into Florida to put down the Seminoles. In this the First Seminole War (1817–1818), Jackson and his men destroyed Seminole villages and crushed the resistance. The soldiers also invaded the Florida city of Pensacola and took it from the Spanish.

One year later, the United States purchased Florida from Spain. U.S. merchants and farmers came to settle the new territory. Clashes with the Seminoles soon followed. Trying to restore order, the governor of Florida persuaded the Seminoles to sign a treaty. According to this document, the Seminoles agreed to move to an area in central Florida. This area was one of the first reservations—land specifically set aside for Indians—in the United States. In exchange for moving, the territorial government promised the Seminole cattle, money, and farming supplies. But the reservation land was sandy and not suitable for farming. It had few edible plants or wild animals for hunting. The promised government supplies never arrived, and many Seminoles began to starve. In response, angry

U.S. slaves escaped to Spanish Florida and sought refuge in Seminole villages like this one. Using the excuse of quelling a U.S. slave rebellion in the Spanish territory, Jackson and 3,000 army troops entered Florida in 1817. They finally defeated Seminole and African American fighters there in 1818.

Seminole warriors began to raid white settlements.

In 1828 Andrew Jackson became president of the United States. In his annual message to Congress in 1830, Jackson clearly spelled out his vision for the United States—a vision in which white society had replaced Indian society. He asked: "What good man would prefer a country covered with forests and ranged by a few thousand savages to our extensive Republic, studded with cities, towns, and prosperous farms, embellished with all the improvements which art can devise or industry execute, occupied by more than 12,000,000 happy people, and filled with all the blessings of liberty, civilization, and religion?"

That same year, Congress passed the Indian Removal Act, which called for the relocation of all eastern Indian nations west of the Mississippi River. Backed by federal law, U.S. soldiers began rounding up entire nations and escorting them to what is now Oklahoma, which had been designated as Indian Territory.

In Florida some Seminoles refused to leave their homeland. Their resistance led to the Second Seminole War (1835–1842). As fighters, the Seminoles were highly skilled and difficult to defeat. They had a courageous leader named Osceola. He and his warriors picked off U.S. soldiers in surprise ambushes, then slipped into swamps to hide. After battles, they scattered and disappeared.

> **EYEWITNESS QUOTE: OSCEOLA'S PERSPECTIVE**
>
> "You have guns, and so have we. You have men and so have we. Your men will fight and so will ours until the last drop of the Seminole's blood has moistened the dust of his hunting ground."
>
> —Osceola to U.S. settlers, 1836

In the fall of 1837, the U.S. Army commander in Florida, Thomas Jesup, asked Osceola to meet with him under a flag of truce (a temporary cease-fire). When Osceola arrived, soldiers seized him and held him captive. Osceola became ill during his captivity. He suffered with malaria and a throat disease for three months. On January 30, 1838, he rose from his sickbed, pulled on his battle dress, and applied war paint to his face. Lying down again, Osceola took out his scalping knife, laid his arms across his chest, and died.

Osceola's people were outraged at the treachery of the U.S. forces. They continued to resist the forced occupation of their lands. When U.S. forces burned their villages,

This 1838 George Catlin painting is of Osceola shortly before his death. Osceola led the Seminole people against U.S. forces during the Second Seminole War.

they hid in woods and swamps. A new U.S. commander, Colonel Zachary Taylor, was fierce in his determination to squelch Seminole resistance. He even used bloodhounds to locate them, but the Indians still would not surrender. After years of brave resistance, the Seminoles were finally defeated in 1842 and were moved to Indian Territory.

Although most Seminoles relocated, some—led by Chief Boleck—hid in the Everglades, a vast swamp in southern Florida. In 1855 white settlers stole some crops belonging to the Seminoles. The Indians demanded either payment or an apology. They received neither, and this incident led to a Third Seminole War (1855–1858). Again, U.S. forces prevailed, and the Indians surrendered. Most of them, including Chief Boleck and his followers, were moved to Indian Territory.

THE BLACK HAWK WAR

While the Seminoles were struggling to hold on to their land, Indian nations farther north also clashed with the U.S. Army. The Meskwakis, meaning "red earth people," were an Algonquian nation. French fur traders called them the Fox. They had first lived in Michigan and Wisconsin. Later, they settled around Illinois, on both banks of the Mississippi River. In 1733 they merged with a nearby Algonquian nation called the Sauks.

In 1804 U.S. government agents invited several Sauk and Fox chiefs to a party. The Indians were encouraged to get drunk. Once drunk, they signed a treaty that they were told allowed whites to hunt on

Artist J. O. Lewis created this painting of Ma-ka-ta-i-me-she-kia-kiak (Black Hawk) in 1834. Black Hawk, along with other leaders, was tricked into signing a treaty that granted the U.S. government millions of acres of Sauk and Meskwaki (Fox) land. Black Hawk declared the treaty invalid and organized his people to defend their homeland.

Indian land. In actuality, the treaty gave 50 million acres of land east of the Mississippi River to the United States. Later, a chief wrote: "I [signed] . . . the treaty not knowing that by that act, I consented to give away my village."

The Sauk leader who wrote those words was named Black Hawk. He was a medicine man, a warrior, and a respected leader. When Black Hawk realized what the treaty really said, he declared it to be invalid. He then fought alongside the British in the War of 1812.

In the years that followed, as he watched white settlers move onto his people's land,

Black Hawk's bitterness grew. In 1831, after a winter spent hunting to the west, Black Hawk led his people back to their village, Saukenauk (present-day Rock Island, Illinois), at crop-planting time. They found white settlers living and farming there. One family had taken over Black Hawk's house. Black Hawk protested to the U.S. government, but his protest was ignored. Even worse, the government announced that the land in question was going to be put up for public sale.

In April 1832, after a trip west, Black Hawk crossed the Mississippi River with 1,000 men, women, and children and headed toward his village. The white settlers living there feared the Indians would attack. They asked the U.S. government for protection. The U.S. Army sent 275 men, led by Major Isaiah Stillman.

In May, Stillman's forces caught up with Black Hawk. Away from his main camp, Black Hawk had only forty warriors with him. He decided to surrender and sent out messengers under a flag of truce. But Stillman's men ignored the flag and fired upon the delegation. Three Sauk fell dead. Black Hawk was enraged. Although he knew his small force did not stand a chance against the U.S. soldiers, and thinking he was certainly going to his death, he led his men in a charge. To Black Hawk's surprise, Stillman's men turned and fled from his warriors.

Black Hawk continued his resistance. He led his warriors in raids on white settlements. His men killed and scalped victims. The settlers were angry. A newspaper editor in Illinois demanded a "war of extermination until there shall be no Indian . . . left." Volunteer soldiers rushed to join the fight against Black Hawk.

Soon, the Sauk chief found himself surrounded by troops on every side. More than half his warriors had been killed. On August 3, 1832, while camped on the banks of the Bad Axe River in Wisconsin, Black Hawk, his remaining warriors, and their families tried to surrender to nearby U.S. soldiers. But instead of accepting the surrender, the soldiers set upon the Indians without mercy. They shot, stabbed, and clubbed men, women, and children. A steamboat that was

This painting, created by Wisconsin artist Cal Peters in the mid-1900s, depicts the slaughter of the Sauk Indians as they fled U.S. Army troops during the Battle of Bad Axe in 1832.

being used as a warship turned its cannons upon the Indians. Almost 300 Sauk and Fox people were killed in the massacre.

Black Hawk managed to escape with a few followers. He tried to find refuge with the Ho-Chunk Nation, but they turned him over to the U.S. authorities for a reward of $100 and twenty horses. "Black Hawk is now a prisoner of the white man," he declared, "but he . . . is not afraid of death. He is no coward. Black Hawk is an Indian." The Sauk and Fox people were resettled on a reservation in Iowa, where Black Hawk died.

THE TRAIL OF TEARS

Unlike some other Indian nations, the Cherokees tried to live peacefully with the white newcomers. They had signed many treaties with the U.S. government. They even adopted some European ways: they ran sawmills, used machines to weave cotton, and built many miles of roads. A young Cherokee named Sequoyah created a system for writing the Cherokee language. Cherokee children attended school and learned to read and write. The nation even published its own newspaper, the *Cherokee Phoenix*.

The Cherokees were a self-governing society. They elected a chief and a legislature that met in their capital city of New Echota, Georgia. In 1827 the nation created a written constitution. Yet not all Cherokees accepted the wisdom of following white ways. Some felt that "the Great Spirit is displeased with [the Cherokees] for accepting the ways of the white people."

In all, the Cherokees occupied about seven million acres of fertile land in the Southeast. As more white settlers arrived in the region, they began to greedily eye Cherokee territory. In 1819 the state of Georgia tried to purchase the land, but the Cherokee Nation refused. Cherokee chiefs passed a law forbidding such sales.

In 1828 gold was discovered at the edge of Cherokee territory. White Americans wanted

Native American Profile: The Cherokees

The Cherokee people have had many homelands. Thousands of years ago, their ancestors lived in present-day Texas. Then they migrated to the Great Lakes region. There, they frequently warred with their neighbors, the more powerful Iroquois and Delawares, who eventually pushed the Cherokees south again. They finally settled in the valleys of the Allegheny and Appalachian mountain ranges, mostly in present-day Tennessee, Georgia, and Alabama.

Historically, the Cherokees lived in permanent villages, where they grew corn, beans, and squash. Women farmed and gathered wild plants. Men hunted deer, bears, and elk. They grew tobacco to smoke during sacred rituals.

Cherokee life changed with the seasons. The warm season between April and October was time to travel, plant, harvest, and go to war. The cold season from October to April was time to collect nuts, hunt for game, and tell stories.

the gold (and land) for themselves. The Georgia legislature passed several laws designed to take Cherokee lands for the state. The Cherokees appealed to the U.S. government, citing earlier treaties that had given the land to them. But President Andrew Jackson sided with the Georgia lawmakers.

The Indian Removal Act, passed in 1830, set a deadline of May 23, 1838, for the removal of the Cherokee and other southeastern Native American nations to Indian

The Bureau of Indian Affairs

To handle interactions with Indian tribes and nations, the U.S. government created the Bureau of Indian Affairs in 1824. The bureau was first part of the War Department (the present-day Department of Defense) and was transferred to the Department of the Interior in 1849. The bureau's first job was to oversee existing treaties with Native American nations and to negotiate new ones. The bureau's agents also ran Indian reservations. Many agents were Christian missionaries who tried to persuade Indians to give up their traditional customs in favor of Christianity and other white institutions.

Some Indian agents were honest, capable, and respected by Native Americans. Many others, however, were dishonest. They made illegal deals, such as selling government supplies that were meant for Native Americans, or allowing big companies to cut timber or dig for minerals on reservations lands. Corruption in the Indian Bureau was widespread and well known in the 1800s, but the U.S. government made few efforts to reform the bureau or punish dishonest agents.

Territory. The Cherokees tried all legal means to fight this act but were defeated each time. By 1835 some Cherokees were tired of the ongoing struggle. Under pressure to make a deal, 500 Cherokee leaders signed a treaty with the U.S. government, agreeing to give up their territory. In exchange, they received $5,700,000 and land in Indian Territory in the West.

Most Cherokees had opposed the treaty, and 16,000 of them signed a petition addressed to their leaders stating their opposition. But their pleas were ignored. U.S. troops began to force the Cherokees off their land. When the deadline for removal arrived in May 1838, 18,000 to 20,000 Cherokees were still clinging to their homes.

General Winfield Scott commanded the U.S. troops charged with removing the Cherokees. Scott told his soldiers that the Indians should be treated kindly. But his soldiers ignored this order. Some robbed and murdered Cherokees as they rounded them up. Men, women, and children were shoved into crude, disease-ridden camps in Georgia and kept there throughout the summer. Many starved, fell ill, and died.

In autumn the forced march to Oklahoma began. Driven along by soldiers, the Cherokees left their homeland, traveling in several different groups along three different routes. The lucky ones traveled by wagon. Most walked the roughly 1,200 miles, which came to be called the Trail of Tears. The march lasted through the cold, rainy fall and winter months of 1838 and 1839. Four thousand Cherokee died along the way. They were buried in shallow graves by the roadside.

NATIVE AMERICAN STEREOTYPES

Like President Andrew Jackson, most white Americans of the 1800s wanted to eliminate Indians from the United States. Jackson's view was based on political considerations. He believed, as did many white leaders of the time, that independent, self-governing Indian peoples within U.S. borders were a threat to the United States. As president, Jackson signed the Indian Removal Act of 1830, which forced Native Americans to give up their land in the East and move west of the Mississippi.

The average white American, however, did not think of Native Americans as a political problem. Most whites viewed Indians as ignorant, bloodthirsty "savages" who had no right to the land they inhabited. What's more, many white Americans believed in manifest destiny, the idea that God wanted the United States to stretch from the Atlantic to the Pacific oceans. Native Americans stood in the way of this vision and, according to many whites, had to be removed through force.

Settlers justified the policy of killing and relocating Indians by portraying them in a negative way. For instance, Lewis Cass, who forced Native Americans off huge tracts of land when he was governor of the Michigan Territory, proclaimed that Indians were "a barbarous people" who "cannot live in contact with a civilized community." Books and magazine articles also encouraged this view of Native Americans as wild and primitive. Some writers vividly pictured innocent white pioneers being hacked to death and scalped by vicious Indians armed with tomahawks. Others told tales of brave U.S. cavalrymen battling "savages" to defend settlers. Newspaper reports exaggerated the atrocities of Indians, creating outrage that led whites to call for revenge. *The Last of the Mohicans* (1826), a novel by the popular writer James Fenimore Cooper, portrayed Mohican Indians as noble (another stereotype) but showed other Native American peoples to be bloodthirsty.

At the other extreme, but just as damaging, was the portrayal of Native Americans as ignorant and immature. White leaders frequently referred to Indians as children. The president of the United States was their "white father," government agents told the Indians. Indians were also the objects of curiosity and amusement. Buffalo Bill's Wild West Show, a popular touring pageant, operated during the late 1800s under brightly colored circus tents. The show enacted exaggerated dramas about western life, such as cowboy and Indian battles, buffalo hunts, and Indian raids on stagecoaches. Such acts spread the picture of Native Americans as a savage race that rode wildly across the plains.

These images of Native Americans continued into the 1900s and were reinforced by movies. In typical 20th-century Westerns, Native Americans were the villains, who were defeated in the end by the brave white heroes. Only in recent decades, have some films begun to show the point of view of Native Americans.

WARS IN THE WEST— PART ONE

After purchasing more than 825,000 square miles of territory from France in the Louisiana Purchase of 1803, Thomas Jefferson sent an expedition to explore the new territory and to find a passage across the continent to the Pacific Ocean. Army officers Meriwether Lewis and William Clark headed the expedition. They traveled along rivers, over mountains, and through forests to map the wilderness. Pioneers and adventurers soon followed in the path set by Lewis and Clark, looking for opportunities and riches in the vast, open spaces of North America.

Jefferson had a vision of the United States extending across the entire continent. By the 1830s, political leaders and journalists were using a term, *manifest destiny,* to describe Jefferson's dream. Americans who believed in manifest destiny felt it was God's will for the United States to control the whole continent, from the Atlantic Ocean to the Pacific Ocean. The U.S. government encouraged farmers and ranchers to settle the West, on "empty" land waiting to be developed.

Thousands of settlers traveled west along the Oregon Trail, an overland route that started in Independence, Missouri. The trail extended 2,000 miles along raging rivers, over rugged mountains, through valleys, and across narrow canyons, ending at the Columbia River in Oregon. With their possessions loaded into covered wagons, travelers on the trail faced dangers such as harsh weather, epidemics of disease, wild animals, and Indian raids. Altogether, about 350,000 travelers headed west across the Oregon Trail. A number of other trails also led west. The hardy pioneers who survived the overland journey built farms and towns in the rich western lands.

But the western lands were not unoccupied. They were home to thousands of Native Americans. The western Indian nations, including the Cayuses, Bannocks, and Shoshones of Oregon and Idaho, the Utes of Nevada and Utah, and the Apaches and Navajos of the Southwest, knew what had happened to Indian nations in the East. They wanted to avoid the same fate. The whites' philosophy of manifest destiny and the Indians' determination to resist that destiny, again resulted in warfare.

WAR WITH THE CAYUSES

One of the first Indian Wars in the West occurred along the Oregon-Washington border. Marcus and Narcissa Whitman, Presbyterian missionaries, had settled there among the Cayuse people in 1836. The Whitmans set up a mission (religious complex) on the banks of the Walla Walla River. They lived there among the Cayuse at a settlement called Waiilatpu, which means "the place of the rye grass."

For ten years, the Whitmans and other white missionaries tried to convert local Indians to Christianity.

Believing their own religion was superior to Indian beliefs, the missionaries frequently insulted and offended their Cayuse neighbors. Resentment toward the missionaries grew.

In 1847 a wagon train of white settlers passed through the area and spread an epidemic of measles among the Cayuses. Almost half the nation died. The surviving members blamed the Whitmans for the epidemic, believing the couple had deliberately poisoned them in order to seize their land. In November, led by their chief, Tilokaikt, the Cayuses attacked the mission. They murdered 10 white missionaries, including the Whitmans. Dozens more were taken captive.

The white citizens of the territory were outraged. They called for a militia to avenge the killings. Colonel Cornelius Gilliam headed this force of 550 citizen-soldiers. In January 1848, he led his troops up the Columbia River. They destroyed a Cayuse camp, killing dozens of men, women, and children—innocent people who had had no part in Chief Tilokaikt's raid.

The territorial governor appointed a peace commission to settle the dispute with the Cayuses, but Colonel Gilliam wanted no part of peace talks. He was determined to defeat Native Americans in the area. A week later, his troops battled with warriors from another tribe, the Palouses. The struggle lasted all day. Ten of Gilliam's men were hurt. Gilliam decided his army should retreat to Waiilatpu.

> **EYEWITNESS QUOTE: THE LEGACY OF A PEOPLE**
>
> "When the last red man shall have perished, and the memory of my tribe shall have become a myth among the white men, these shores will swarm with the invisible dead of my tribe."
>
> —Seattle, chief of the Duwamish people

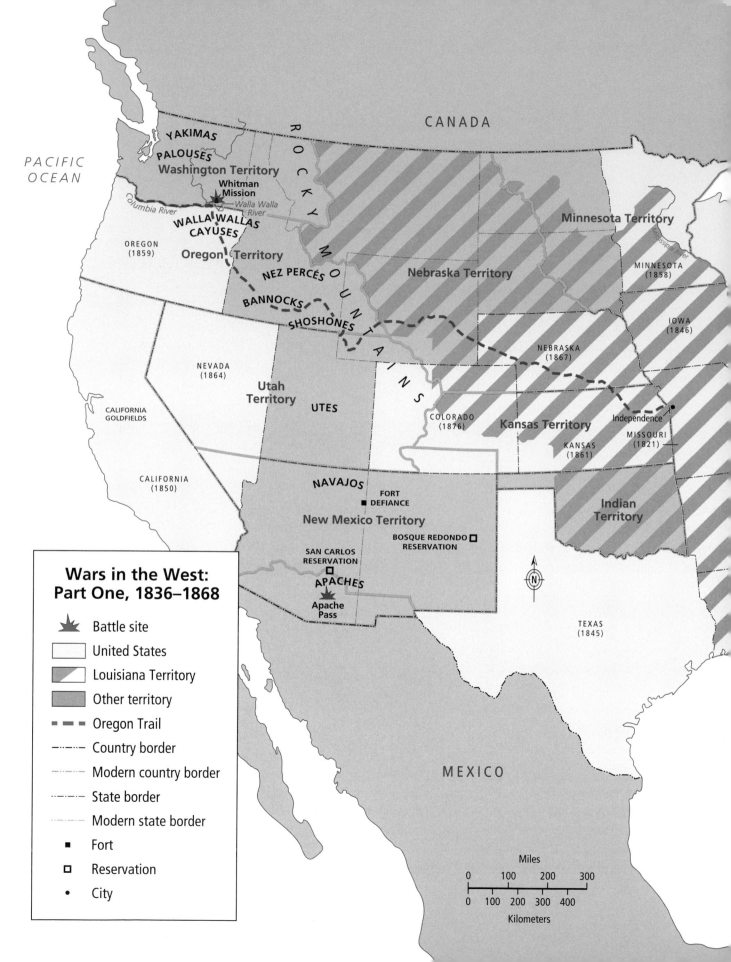

CANADA

PACIFIC
OCEAN

YAKIMAS
PALOUSES
Washington Territory
Whitman
Mission
Walla Walla
River
Columbia River
WALLA WALLAS
CAYUSES
Oregon Territory
OREGON
(1859)
NEZ PERCÉS
BANNOCKS
SHOSHONES

ROCKY MOUNTAINS

Minnesota Territory

MINNESOTA
(1858)

Mississippi River

Nebraska Territory

NEVADA
(1864)

Utah
Territory
UTES

NEBRASKA
(1867)

IOWA
(1846)

CALIFORNIA
GOLDFIELDS

COLORADO
(1876)

Kansas Territory

Independence

MISSOURI
(1821)

CALIFORNIA
(1850)

NAVAJOS
FORT
DEFIANCE

KANSAS
(1861)

New Mexico Territory
BOSQUE REDONDO
RESERVATION

SAN CARLOS
RESERVATION
APACHES
Apache
Pass

Indian
Territory

N

TEXAS
(1845)

MEXICO

**Wars in the West:
Part One, 1836–1868**

⚝ Battle site

▭ United States

▨ Louisiana Territory

▨ Other territory

▬ ▬ ▬ Oregon Trail

–··–··– Country border

–···–···– Modern country border

–·–·– State border

–··–··– Modern state border

■ Fort

▢ Reservation

• City

Miles
0   100   200   300

0   100   200   300   400
Kilometers

Native American Profile: The Plateau Indians

The Plateau Indians occupied the lands of the far Northwest, including Idaho, eastern Oregon and Washington, and western Montana. The area's mountains, valleys, and rivers were natural barriers against enemies.

Plateau tribes and nations included the Nez Percés, Cayuses, Walla Wallas, Ootlashoots, Yakimas, and others. The people were hunters and gatherers. In the spring, the women dug edible roots while the men hunted rabbits and netted fish from rivers. Summer was the season of plenty. The rivers swarmed with fish and other animals. In the fall, hunting teams stalked deer, elk, buffalo, and other big game. Winter was a time for staying at home in villages. Women wove baskets. Men played games and passed on sacred stories to young people.

The militia continued to raid Indian settlements. In response, the local peoples, including the Walla Walla, Palouse, and Nez Perce, were ready to unite in a war against white settlers. The territorial government managed to avoid all-out war by ordering the militia to stop the raids in June 1848. But anger and mistrust between settlers and their Native American neighbors continued.

GOLD RUSHES

In 1848 gold was discovered in northern California. The gold rush was on. Anyone able to reach the goldfields and stake a claim could become rich. People from every walk of life set forth on the perilous journey to the West Coast. Thousands traveled along the Oregon Trail and other routes west. As the gold seekers feverishly rushed to stake claims, many Native Americans in California were killed and forced off their lands.

To the north, in Oregon, the territorial government opened up all land to homesteading in 1850. Homesteading meant that white settlers could set down stakes and claim western land as their own. The territorial government did not recognize any Native American rights to the land. In 1855 miners discovered more gold on the upper Columbia River in Washington State. This discovery brought another

Miners use a sluice, or water trough, to sift gold from gravel in California during the 1800s. The discovery of gold in the West brought thousands of people to the region and onto Native American lands.

stampede of white miners and settlers to the Northwest.

As in other places, white newcomers viewed Indians as an obstacle to their prosperity. To remove Indians from the lands they wanted, leaders in Washington Territory passed a law creating reservations for local Native Americans. U.S. soldiers set about rounding up and relocating Indians onto these reservations. Some nations, such as the Yakimas, resisted. Battles raged until 1858, when the Yakimas were defeated and moved to reservations.

NAVAJOS AND APACHES AT WAR

The Navajo and Apache were the most powerful and warlike Indian nations of the Southwest. They lived in harsh country— the hot, dry deserts and barren mountains of Arizona, New Mexico, and western Texas. These nations had first come to fear and distrust white people in the 1500s, when Spanish explorers came to their lands, searching for gold. The Navajo and Apaches fought off attacks by Spanish and later Mexican soldiers. For 150 years, Indians and Mexicans frequently raided each other's towns and villages.

The United States and Mexico fought the Mexican War (1846–1848) over disputed borders between Texas and Mexico. The United States was victorious. As a result, Mexico was forced to give up hundreds of thousands of square miles of southwestern land, all of it already inhabited by Native Americans.

During and after the Mexican War, the U.S. Army built forts all around the newly acquired southwestern territory. The forts were constructed to protect settlers from Navajo and Apache warriors, who were known to be ferocious fighters. One of the most powerful Indian leaders was Mangas Coloradas of the Mescalero Apaches. Mangas was a large man and was greatly admired for his courage and intelligence. By 1861 he was 70 years old but still a tough warrior. A young warrior named Cochise, chief of the Chiricahua Apaches, was one of Mangas's allies.

General Winfield Scott *(center on horseback)* leads victorious U.S. soldiers into Mexico City near the end of the Mexican War in 1847. The U.S. victory meant that Indian lands in the southwest once held but only lightly settled by Mexico became part the United States.

Reservation Life

In the early 1800s, as part of its Indian policy, the U.S. government began to create reservations. In this way, the government thought it could control and contain Indians as well as seize their lands for white settlement. One of the first reservations was established in central Florida, after the First Seminole War in 1818.

Reservations varied in size, from only a handful of acres to millions of acres. Where resources were available, reservation Indians supported themselves by hunting, farming, and fishing. They built traditional homes out of animal hides and plant materials, similar to those they had always used. But reservation Indians were under the control of the U.S. government. Soldiers at nearby forts made sure that Indians stayed on the reservation.

As white settlers pushed westward and took over more and more land, the U.S. government moved Native Americans to smaller reservations on less desirable lands—barren stretches without much wildlife or good farmland. Because Indians could not hunt, grow, or gather much food on such lands, they became dependent on government shipments of food and other necessities for their survival. In 1878 General George Crook wrote in the *Army and Navy Journal* about a reservation for Bannock Indians: "The buffalo [are] all gone, and an Indian can't catch enough jack rabbits to [feed] himself and his family. . . . Starvation is staring them in the face." Epidemics of disease frequently swept through the reservations.

By the mid-1880s, approximately 243,000 Indians were living on 187 reservations, most of them west of the Mississippi River. Indian agents, employees of the Bureau of Indian Affairs, oversaw day-to-day life on the reservation. A few Indians were given jobs as reservation police officers. But for the most part, Indian residents had no voice in how reservations operated. They had no right to vote or freedom to leave the reservation. They were not even considered citizens of the United States.

To try to get Indians to live like white Americans, the bureau sent white farmers and carpenters to reservations to teach Indians modern farming and building methods. The bureau also built schoolhouses and sent teachers to the reservations. Missionaries also worked on reservations, teaching Indians about Christianity. In most cases, Indian religious ceremonies were banned.

In 1887, in another effort to encourage Indians to behave like white people, as well as to free up reservation lands for private ownership, Congress passed the Dawes Act. The act broke up some reservations into small parcels. Then the government gave plots of up to 160 acres to Indian families, who were encouraged to farm the land. But Indians had no tradition of small family farms and no interest in living like white people. What's more, much of the land allotted under the Dawes Act was unsuitable for farming. Many Indians sold their lands to white farmers and returned to reservations.

Cochise and Jeffords: Friendship amid Warfare

Among white settlers and traders, Cochise and his warriors were greatly feared. So it was a surprise in 1867 when a white man walked boldly into Cochise's tent. The man was Thomas Jeffords. He operated a mail route by wagon through Apache territory, but Apache raids made it nearly impossible to do his job.

Cochise was impressed by Jeffords's courage. He ordered his men never to attack Jeffords's mail wagons. After that, Jeffords often visited Cochise's camp. The two men became good friends. The Apaches gave Jeffords the name Taglito, which means "red beard" (Jeffords had a red beard). In 1872 Jeffords helped convince Cochise to make a peace treaty with the U.S. Army.

"Cochise, 1877," the earliest painting of the chief known to exist

Together, Mangas Coloradas and Cochise raided settlements in Mexico, but until February 1861, they left U.S. settlers in peace. That year, however, a U.S. Army officer falsely accused Cochise of raiding a white man's ranch and kidnapping his son. Cochise met with the officer, Second Lieutenant George N. Bascom, at a stagecoach station called Apache Pass in Arizona. Cochise thought the meeting would be peaceful, and he brought along several of his relatives. He politely denied the charge against him. He even offered to help get the boy back from the kidnappers.

Bascom did not believe Cochise. He tried to arrest him, but the Apache chief slashed an opening in the tent where they had been meeting and escaped. Cochise's companions were not as lucky. They were arrested and held as hostages. Angrily, Cochise and his warriors captured three white civilians and offered to exchange them for the Apache prisoners. Bascom refused, so Cochise tortured and killed his prisoners. In return, Bascom hanged Cochise's relatives.

After this incident, Cochise and his ally Mangas led their warriors in attacks on wagon trains, settlements, and U.S. soldiers. They hoped to drive all white people from the Apache homelands.

By this time, the Civil War (1861–1865) was raging between the Northern and Southern states. The war took place primarily east of the Mississippi River, but some fighting spilled over into western territories. A Union (Northern) general named James Henry Carleton commanded an army in California known as the California Column. Early in 1862, he led his unit to New Mexico to drive off Confederate (Southern) troops in the area. On the way, they passed through Apache lands in Arizona. The army needed water. When they neared Apache Pass on July 15, 1862, Carleton sent some soldiers ahead to look for springs. Led by Captain Thomas L. Roberts, the group consisted of an infantry company (foot soldiers), seven cavalrymen on horseback, and two wagons containing huge cannons called howitzers.

Artists Look at Native Americans

The way white artists depicted Native Americans usually reflected how white society as a whole thought of them. This view changed over time. One idea popular in the 1700s and early 1800s was that of the Indian as "noble savage"—uncorrupted, heroic, wild, and free. This type of image can be seen in the paintings of Charles Bird King. In the 1820s, King went to work for the newly formed Bureau of Indian Affairs, painting portraits of Native American chiefs who visited Washington, D.C. In the course of about 20 years, King painted the likenesses of 140 chiefs.

A Native American shaman of the Great Plains as portrayed by George Catlin.

In 1832 George Catlin, a young Philadelphia lawyer-turned-painter, became the first white artist to travel west with the sole purpose of meeting and portraying Native Americans as they lived. He followed the route of Lewis and Clark's expedition and documented the many bands of Plains Indians he encountered. He meticulously noted their customs and rituals in his notebook as he painted and sketched. Like King, Catlin showed Indians to be noble and heroic.

Other artists showed Native Americans as cruel and bloodthirsty—a view held by many in white society. This image first appeared with John Vanderlyn's *The Murder of Jane McCrea* (1804), a frightening depiction of a real event. Later artists created similar views of Indians as ferocious and savage. Examples include *Osage Scalp Dance* (1845) by John Mix Stanley and *The Death Struggle* (1845) by Charles Deas. Finally, as the United States succeeded in subduing the Indians, images of Native Americans as a tragic, defeated, and "doomed" people began to appear. The first such work was Tompkins Matteson's *The Last of the Race* (1847).

As for Native Americans themselves, scholars claim there is no word for *art* in any Native American language. But all Native American groups have vibrant artistic traditions. Native people have long created beautiful everyday objects, such as baskets, blankets, pottery, and jewelry. When millions of buffalo roamed across the Great Plains, native artists painted pictures of humans and animals on buffalo hides.

With the destruction of the buffalo in the late 1800s, buffalo hides became scarce. At the same time, more and more Native Americans were being moved to reservations. There, Indians began making drawings on paper, using colored pencils, paint, and charcoal provided by Indian agents. Known as ledger drawings, many of these works depicted the past glories of Indian culture and the sad story of Indian removal. In the 1900s, several Native Americans became well-known artists. This group includes Fred Kabotie, T. C. Cannon, R. C. Gorman, and Fritz Scholder.

WOMEN IN THE INDIAN WARS

Women rarely took part in battles during the Indian Wars. Occasionally, white women traveled with the troops, acting as cooks, nurses, and laundresses, but they were not part of organized units or nursing corps. Many women—both white and Indian—were victims of the wars, however. Sometimes, U.S. soldiers would raid Indian villages or Indian warriors would attack white settlements. In both cases, everyone in sight, including women and children, risked being slaughtered.

Native American Women Most Native American women had no training as warriors. They were expected to raise crops, manage the household, and care for children, but not to fight. Often Native American women tended the injured after a battle. They would bind up wounds and treat them with medicines made from roots and herbs.

But some women of the Plains nations did become fighters. Called many-hearted women, they were known to charge enemies in combat. One of these was Buffalo Calf Woman. In the summer of 1876, she rushed onto a battlefield to fight and rescue her injured brother. Ehyophsta, the daughter of a Cheyenne chief, was another Native American heroine. She was called Yellow-Haired Woman, and she fought in many battles against other rival Indian peoples, as well as against the U.S. Army.

White Women White women, especially on isolated farms or ranches, sometimes learned to use firearms to defend themselves from Indian raids. Many stories tell of frontier women fighting savagely to protect their homes and families. Women who lived in large settlements or towns generally did not confront raiders.

White women were frequently taken prisoner by warriors during the Indian Wars. In 1697 Hannah Dustin used a tomahawk to kill her Indian captors and free herself after a raid on her Massachusetts town. Other white women lived with Indians who captured them. Some women adapted well to Indian life and even refused to return to their homes when given the chance. Those who did return were often looked down upon by their white neighbors.

Meanwhile, Mangas and Cochise had hidden 500 warriors on the rocky heights above the pass. As Roberts's troops entered Apache Pass, a deadly hail of arrows and bullets flew at them. The soldiers retreated. Then they returned with their howitzers. Once again, the Apaches aimed and fired. Suddenly, the two wagons thundered with the roar of fire from the howitzers. Warriors fell by the dozens. The survivors retreated.

In January 1863, after another raid on U.S. troops, army officers invited Mangas to a "peace conference" at an army camp. But the meeting was a trick. U.S. soldiers arrested Mangas and then murdered him. Cochise and the other Apaches were enraged. "The Indians went to war in earnest, . . . " said one observer. "They seemed bent on avenging [Mangas's] death with all their power."

The Apaches began a campaign of terror, slaughtering white travelers and raiding white settlements, that lasted for years.

But the Apaches were few in number. Gradually, U.S. forces defeated them. One by one, Indian leaders asked for peace.

Finally, in 1872, Cochise signed a treaty with the U.S. government. With this treaty, the Apaches agreed to move to a reservation. But Cochise insisted that the reservation be near the Apache homeland in southeastern Arizona. "When I was young I walked all over this country. . . . " Cochise noted sadly. "The Apaches were once a great nation; they are now but few."

Cochise died in 1874. The next year, the Bureau of Indian Affairs ordered the Apaches moved north to the San Carlos Reservation in east-central Arizona. San Carlos was hot and barren, with many disease-carrying insects. Some Apaches refused to stay on the reservation and were able to escape to freedom. Their new leader was a Chiricahua Apache chief named Goyathlay. He was better known by his Mexican name—Geronimo.

This group of Apache Indians (left) was photographed on a reservation in Arizona during the 1870s. Many Apache people, like the men on horseback at right, refused to live on reservations.

Warrior chief Geronimo *(front row, third from right)* led a group of Apache freedom fighters in the 1880s. The warriors resisted U.S. efforts to force the Apache people onto reservations. Geronimo is shown here with other Apaches shortly after their capture in late 1886.

In the 1880s, Geronimo led his Apache warriors in daring raids upon settlers and U.S. Army troops. But weakened by U.S. Army attacks, Geronimo's forces surrendered to General Nelson A. Miles in late 1886. The Apaches, including Geronimo, were moved once more, carried by train to a reservation in Florida. The Apaches were miserable in this unfamiliar territory. Many of them were allowed to move back west as far as Oklahoma. There, on a reservation, Geronimo lived out the last years of his life.

THE LONG MARCH OF THE NAVAJO

The Navajos, like the Apaches, were a large and prosperous nation. In the early 1800s, 12,000 Navajos lived in the Southwest. When the Mexican War ended in 1848, Navajo lands in New Mexico and Arizona became part of the United States.

At first, Navajo leaders thought they could live in peace with white Americans and made treaties with them. "Our fathers . . . heard that the Americans were coming across the great river," Navajo chief Manuelito related. "We heard of guns and powder and lead. . . . When the Americans first came we had a big dance and . . . traded."

Soon, whites and Navajos began to argue over territory. The U.S. Army built a settlement in Arizona called Fort Defiance and grazed their horses on nearby Indian land. They ordered the Navajos to keep their own horses off these pastures. When Indian horses wandered near Fort Defiance, soldiers shot and killed them. The shootings led to a series of raids on villages and forts by both Navajos and U.S. soldiers.

In April 1860, two Navajo chiefs, Manuelito and Barboncito, led 1,000 warriors in an attack upon Fort Defiance. At first, the Navajos seemed to have the upper hand, and the soldiers fled. They soon regrouped, however, and launched a steady barrage of musket fire against the warriors. The Navajos had to pull back into the hills.

More battles followed as the U.S. Army chased Manuelito across the countryside. Finally, in January 1861, the two sides signed a peace treaty. For a short period, Navajos and whites traded with one another. They even competed in horse races. During one race, Navajo spectators accused a white rider of slashing the reins of an Indian rider. A fight broke out, and Navajo women and children were killed. After this incident, hostilities resumed.

In the spring of 1862, General Carleton turned his attention from the Apaches to the Navajos. His aim was to drive them off their land to open it up for white settlement. Carleton sent a message to the Navajos, commanding them to report to U.S. forts and from there to be sent to a reservation. "Tell them they can have until the twentieth day of July . . . to come in . . . ," he ordered. "After that day every Navajo that is seen will be considered as hostile and treated accordingly." Carleton's order continued. "There is to be no council [meeting] held with the Indians. . . . The men are to be slain whenever and wherever they can be found."

Carleton placed Colonel Kit Carson and his regiment in charge of enforcing this order. Under Carleton's orders, Carson raided Navajo villages. Most villagers managed to escape and hide in nearby mountains, canyons, and valleys. The villagers were weakened by Carson's frequent attacks but continued to resist. So Carleton then ordered Carson and his troops to destroy the Navajos' means of survival—their crops of corn, wheat, fruit, and melons. The soldiers also stole or killed herds of Navajo goats and sheep. Soon the Navajos had no food to eat and no way to earn a living. Starving, most of them were forced to surrender.

In the winter of 1864, Carleton had U.S. soldiers march thousands of Navajo men, women, and children across the frozen snow to a reservation called Bosque Redondo in eastern New Mexico. More than 200 Navajos died of exposure, starvation, or disease during what came to be called the Long March. The reservation was bleak. The land there was not suitable for growing crops or herding sheep. The Navajos continued to weaken and die as epidemics of pneumonia and measles swept through the reservation.

In 1868 a group of Navajo leaders went to Washington, D.C., to describe the suffering of their people to President Andrew Johnson. Word spread about the terrible conditions at Bosque Redondo. As a result, the government allowed the Navajos to move to a new reservation on their traditional lands on the New Mexico–Arizona border. The Navajos went home, planted crops, and rebuilt their herds.

7 WARS IN THE WEST— PART TWO

For many centuries, independent Indian bands, tribes, and nations lived on the Great Plains of North America. The Great Plains is a vast region of grasslands stretching from south-central Canada to the Mexican border. In the United States, the plains region includes parts of present-day Montana, North and South Dakota, Wyoming, Nebraska, Colorado, Kansas, New Mexico, and Texas. The Indian nations whose historic homelands were on the Great Plains included the Cheyennes, Arapahos, Comanches, Crows, Kiowas, and several groups of Sioux.

Buffalo were essential to the Plains Indians' way of life. Indians depended on buffalo for meat, shelter, tools, and clothing. Some groups hunted buffalo in summer and lived in permanent villages during other seasons. Other groups followed the buffalo herds year-round, moving their tepees from camp to camp as they traveled.

By the mid-1800s, most Indian peoples in the eastern United States had been wiped out, relocated to Indian Territory, or pushed farther west onto the plains. The Native Americans who already lived on the plains resented the newcomers and sometimes warred with them over hunting territory and other resources. These battles weakened all the Indian groups, reducing their numbers of warriors and taking their energy away from hunting.

The Near Extinction of a Species

In 1850 an estimated 20 million buffalo roamed the American plains. White men aggressively hunted buffalo to cripple Native American food supplies, for the animals' hides, and for sport. By 1889 the great herds had dwindled to fewer than 1,000 buffalo. The species was nearly extinct.

Buffalo skinners with roughly 40,000 buffalo hides

White settlers streamed west in great numbers in the mid-1800s. Not only did whites make their new homes and farms on Indian lands, but they also began to kill buffalo. Native hunters also killed buffalo, but they did so for their survival. Little of the animal was wasted: the flesh was used for food, the skins for clothing and tepees, and the bones and horns for tools. In most cases, native hunters killed roughly as many animals as their families or villages needed for survival.

But white buffalo hunters slaughtered animals by the hundreds and thousands. One hunter might kill up to 150 a day. More than 3.5 million were killed between 1872 and 1874 alone. What's more, white hunters didn't use the animals as wisely as Indians did. They shipped the hides back east, where they were made into robes and other luxury items. The bones were ground up into fertilizer. But the dead animals' meat was usually left to rot on the plains. As the buffalo disappeared from the

This Native American ledger artwork, probably created by a Hidatsa Indian, shows a traditional buffalo hunt on the Great Plains.

Wars in the West: Part Two, 1851–1890

- ✴ Battle site
- ☐ United States
- Other territory
- – – – Oregon Trail
- –·–·– Country border
- ——— Modern country border
- –··–··– State border
- –·–·– Modern state border
- ■ Fort
- ☐ Reservation
- ● City

Map labels:
CANADA
PACIFIC OCEAN
WASHINGTON (1889)
Columbia River
BLACKFOOTS
GROS VENTRES
MONTANA (1889)
NORTH DAKOTA (1889)
CROWS
OREGON (1859)
IDAHO (1890)
Battle of the Little Bighorn
STANDING ROCK RESERVATION
SOUTH DAKOTA (1889)
MINNESOTA (1858)
Battle of Rosebud Creek
ARIKARAS
SIOUX
WYOMING (1890)
Wounded Knee Creek Massacre
IOWA
SHOSHONES
CHEYENNES
FORT LARAMIE
Blue Water Creek Massacre
CALIFORNIA
Grattan Massacre
NEBRASKA (1867)
NEVADA (1864)
ARAPAHOS
UTAH (1896)
COLORADO (1876)
Sand Creek Massacre
KANSAS (1861)
Independence
MISSOURI
FORT LYON
KIOWAS
Indian Territory
New Mexico Territory
COMANCHES
TEXAS
MEXICO
Gulf of Mexico
Miles
0 100 200 300
0 100 200 300 400
Kilometers
Mississippi River
ROCKY MOUNTAINS

Great Plains, the Indians who relied on the animals for survival began to increasingly go hungry.

FAILED DIPLOMACY

As in other parts of the United States, government leaders were interested in opening up the lands of the Great Plains for white settlement. Indians wanted to preserve their homelands for themselves. As elsewhere, the two groups sometimes tried to negotiate and other times resorted to violence. Angered at the steady stream of travelers moving through their lands, Indians sometimes attacked whites on the Oregon Trail.

In turn, settlers, soldiers, and others shot and killed Indians.

In 1846 Thomas Fitzpatrick was appointed U.S. Indian agent to the peoples of the plains. He was fair but firm, and the Indians respected him. In September 1851, Fitzpatrick called a meeting of Indian leaders at Fort Laramie in Wyoming. He wanted them to agree to stop attacking travelers along the Oregon Trail. He also wanted the them to make peace with each other, since the frequent warfare between them also made the area unsafe for white travelers. Mostly, Fitzpatrick wanted the Indians to stay in one place. The meeting included chiefs of many tribes and nations of the western plains, including the Cheyennes, Sioux, Arapahos, Shoshones, Arikaras, Crows, and Gros Ventres.

Fitzgerald gave the chiefs gifts and persuaded them to sign treaties. For their part of the bargain, the chiefs agreed to keep their people away from white settlements and wagon trails and within certain boundaries, which meant giving up some of their traditional hunting grounds. In return, Fitzpatrick promised yearly payments of money, food, farm animals, and farm tools.

Fitzpatrick doubted that the treaties would be effective. He knew that many Native American tribes and nations were only loosely united. A few leaders could not speak for all, and those groups that had not attended the meeting could not be expected to follow the agreement. Besides, yearly payments of farm animals and farm tools would not help people who depended

---

APPENDIX.   701

and Fort Laramie, together with communications from the Department of the Interior, and other documents connected therewith.

MILLARD FILLMORE.

WASHINGTON, *February* 13, 1852.

The message was read.

The articles of a treaty made and concluded at Fort Laramie, in the Indian territory, between D. D. Mitchell, superintendent of Indian affairs, and Thomas Fitzpatrick, Indian agent, commissioners specially appointed and authorized by the President of the United States, of the first part, and the chiefs, head-men and braves of the following Indian nations residing south of the Missouri river, east of the Rocky mountains, and north of the lines of Texas and New Mexico, viz: the Sioux or Dah-co-tahs, Cheyennes, Arrapahoes, Crows, Assiniboines, Gros-Ventres, Mandans and Ariccarees, parties of the second part, on the 17th day of September, 1851, were read the first time.

Ordered, That the said treaty, together with the message and documents, be referred to the Committee on Indian Affairs, and printed in confidence for the use of the Senate.

MONDAY, APRIL 19, 1852.

Mr. Atchison, from the Committee on Indian Affairs, to whom was referred, the 17th February last, the treaty with certain Indian tribes at Fort Laramie, on the 17th September, 1851, reported it without amendment.

At left is a congressional report on a treaty between the U.S. government and Native Americans brokered by Thomas Fitzpatrick at Fort Laramie in the mid-1800s.

Native American Profile: The Plains Indians

The Indians of the Great Plains included the Cheyennes, Blackfoots, Arapahos, Comanches, Crows, and several divisions of Sioux. Some groups lived a nomadic lifestyle, following buffalo herds across the plains. Others lived in permanent villages and grew a few crops as well as hunted. The language of the Plains Indians differed, often from group to group. But a common sign language united the peoples with a form of communication.

The Indians of the plains bred swift ponies and were excellent horseback riders. Young men were trained from childhood to be warriors. Pride, courage, and fierceness were greatly admired among the plains peoples.

The Plains Indians worshiped gods related to nature. Some groups believed in an all-powerful creator called the Great Spirit. On special occasions, Plains Indians performed sacred ceremonies that included tobacco smoking. The most important ritual was the Sun Dance. It was performed to give thanks to the Great Spirit and to ask the Great Spirit for help during the coming year. A young man coming of age would go on a sacred "vision quest." For days, he would remain alone, without food or drink, until his mind opened to voices and visions. During this quest, he was expected to see a vision of the spirit that would become his lifetime guardian.

on hunting for survival. Fitzpatrick also realized that many Indian leaders had attended the meeting only for the gifts they had been promised. He warned other white officials that only an effective military force could subdue the Indians. He knew the time would come when U.S. leaders would decide to solve the issue through war.

THE GRATTAN MASSACRE AND BLUE WATER CREEK

Several years of peace followed Fitzpatrick's meeting at Fort Laramie. But grievances remained among the Indians. They decried the loss of their right to hunt and travel wherever they chose. They resented being dependent on yearly payments from the U.S. government. To make matters worse, these payments did not always arrive on time, and government agents and suppliers sometimes stole portions of the payments before they reached Indian families.

As Plains Indians lost their traditional hunting grounds, and as more and more buffalo were slaughtered, many went hungry. On an August day in 1854, a hungry young Lakota Sioux warrior stole a stray ox that had wandered off from a wagon train. He butchered the animal and shared the food with his friends. The white travelers complained to the authorities at Fort Laramie. There, Lieutenant John Grattan gathered a party of 30 soldiers armed with two cannons. They marched to the Lakota camp and demanded that the young men who had eaten the ox be turned over to the army for punishment. The Lakota chief,

Brave Bear, refused. So Grattan ordered his men to open fire on the camp. They killed Brave Bear and several others. Some warriors who had been hiding nearby joined Brave Bear's men in a furious counterattack. They killed Grattan and his entire company.

Settlers and government officials were hungry for revenge. In September 1855, General William S. Harney organized an expedition against the Lakota Sioux. He made no secret of how he planned to deal with the Indians. "By God, I'm for battle—no peace!" he thundered. He marched an army of 600 men along the Oregon Trail to Blue Water Creek in Nebraska, where the Sioux were camped with their new chief, Little Thunder. The Indians were greatly outnumbered. They tried to flee, but Harney's soldiers mowed them down with rifle fire and swords. Eighty-five Lakotas were killed, and seventy women and children were taken captive.

General Harney did not stop with this victory. He led his soldiers in raids throughout Lakota Sioux territory. Lakota chiefs, fearful of Harney's soldiers, agreed to come to Fort Laramie and sign a new treaty. It contained the same terms as the treaty of 1851, with further restrictions on Indian movement.

THE BATTLE OF SAND CREEK

Cheyenne warriors continued to raid white settlements. In 1857 Colonel Edwin V. Sumner led a cavalry force of 300 soldiers against the Cheyennes. Sumner, nicknamed Bull because of his powerful build, battled the Cheyennes on the banks of the Solomon River in western Kansas.

The Cheyenne warriors had prepared by washing their hands in a sacred lake, whose water was supposed to make enemy bullets harmless. But the U.S. soldiers did not use bullets. When Bull Sumner yelled "Charge!" his men drew their sabers (swords) and galloped at the Cheyennes with blades flashing in the sunlight. The Indians fled before the wild charge. Sumner's cavalrymen chased them for seven miles, slashing at the falling warriors.

The Cheyenne warriors lay low for a while. Then they resumed raiding and terrorizing white settlers. In 1864 the governor of Kansas, John Evans, tried unsuccessfully to persuade the Cheyennes to move to a reservation. So the governor resorted to war. He put Colonel John M. Chivington in command of a cavalry force and ordered him to burn villages and kill Cheyennes wherever they were found.

Black Kettle was the leading "peace chief" (peacetime leader) among the Cheyenne bands. He realized his people stood no chance against the might and determination of the U.S. Army. In exchange for a promise of peace, Black Kettle agreed to submit his people to military authority and to move them to a camp in the Sand Creek Valley near Fort Lyon in Colorado. Having agreed to the army's terms, they thought they would be safe there. But Colonel Chivington showed up at the fort and declared he was going to attack Black Kettle. Other officers tried to stop him, but he insisted that it was right and honorable to kill Indians.

Chivington's troops surrounded Black Kettle's village. Black Kettle raised a white flag of surrender, but Chivington ignored it. The troops opened fire and charged. They shot down men, women, and children. They clubbed and scalped their victims. Two hundred Cheyennes were massacred at Sand Creek, most of them women and children. Black Kettle himself escaped death. In spite of the massacre, he continued to work for peace and signed a new treaty with the U.S. government. In it his people gave up all claims to their lands in the Colorado Territory.

As news of the massacre spread across the plains, other chiefs became outraged. Cheyenne, Arapaho, and Lakota Sioux chiefs met in council. They smoked the war pipe, a signal of their determination to unite in war against their common enemy. Bloody raids erupted. Towns were burned and settlers murdered. U.S. soldiers were challenged in furious combat.

When the Civil War ended in 1865, two of the Union's most respected generals took over command of the armies in the West. William Tecumseh Sherman and Philip Henry Sheridan were ruthless soldiers. They resolved to crush Indian resistance once and for all. More army units were sent west, and the tribes and nations of the plains were strong in their resistance. Little by little, however, Indian resistance weakened in the face of the army's greater numbers and larger guns. Many groups eventually signed treaties and were moved into reservations.

CRAZY HORSE AND SITTING BULL

In Dakota and Montana territories, the Lakota Sioux chiefs Crazy Horse and Sitting Bull vowed to continue fighting. They had

The Aftermath of Sand Creek

Although white Americans had long hated and feared Indians, the American public was shocked by the extent of the killings at Sand Creek. A U.S. government committee later investigated the incident. It reported that "from the . . . babe to the old warrior, all who were overtaken were deliberately murdered." Colonel Chivington, who led the massacre, was forced to resign from the army, but he never faced criminal charges for his actions at Sand Creek.

watched the success of the bluecoats as they called the U.S. soldiers (who wore blue uniforms). They knew that a large U.S. force was on its way to apprehend their people and force them onto reservations.

In June 1876, Sitting Bull and Crazy Horse gathered together a large force of Lakota, Cheyenne, and Arapaho warriors on Rosebud Creek in Montana Territory. There, some warriors performed a sacred ceremony called the Sun Dance. During this ritual, Sitting Bull had a vision, or dream. He saw bluecoats "falling like grasshoppers . . . right into the Indian camp"—a sign that the bluecoats would fall in battle.

Chief Sitting Bull

The warriors were prepared to fight. Hundreds of the fighting men rode out from the village at Rosebud Creek, confronting a force of 1,000 U.S. soldiers commanded by General George Crook.

MINORITIES IN THE INDIAN WARS: THE BUFFALO SOLDIERS

Until the Civil War, many African Americans were enslaved. Even those who had their freedom did not have the same rights as white Americans. As a general rule, African Americans were not allowed to serve in the U.S. Army during the 1700s and 1800s. An exception was the Buffalo Soldiers.

On June 18, 1866, the U.S. Congress passed a law creating six regiments of black troops in the U.S. Army. Four of these regiments were infantry (foot soldiers), and two were cavalry (soldiers on horseback). The cavalry units were the Ninth and Tenth Cavalry Regiments.

The Ninth and Tenth Cavalry Regiments played a major part in the history of the West. Until the early 1890s, they made up 20 percent of all cavalry forces on the frontier. The Plains Indians called black cavalrymen Buffalo Soldiers, probably because of their dark curly hair that resembled the hair of buffalo. The black troops were proud to accept this name. Many of them said it was an honor to be compared to the sacred buffalo of the Indians.

The Ninth and Tenth Cavalry Regiments served on the western frontier for more than 20 years. They fought battles with Cheyenne, Arapaho, Comanche, Kiowa, and Apache warriors in Texas, New Mexico, Arizona, Colorado, and the Dakotas. Among the Indian chiefs they faced were Geronimo and Sitting Bull. In addition to fighting, they also built railroads and forts, strung telegraph lines, and protected settlers and wagon trains.

Troops from the Ninth Cavalry were ambushed by Apaches on September 18, 1879, at Las Animas Canyon in New Mexico. A number of soldiers died fighting, and others risked their lives to save their wounded comrades. Five Buffalo Soldiers were awarded the Congressional Medal of Honor for their bravery in this battle.

Buffalo Soldiers of the U.S. Army's 25th Infantry at Fort Keogh, Montana, in 1890. Some of the men are wearing overcoats made from buffalo hide.

Lakota Short Bull created this ledger drawing of the sacred Sun Dance. The U.S. government, fearful of the ceremony's spiritual significance and unifying power, later outlawed its practice.

A battle raged for six hours. The Indians surrounded the U.S. forces, attacking at weak places in the U.S. lines. The Native Americans darted back and forth on horseback, keeping the various army units apart. The tactics worked. Realizing he was outmatched, General Crook and his men retreated to their base camp.

THE BATTLE OF THE LITTLE BIGHORN

While the warriors were celebrating their victory, another U.S. Army unit, led by Lieutenant Colonel George Armstrong Custer, traveled toward the Indian encampment. Custer had 650 men in his Seventh Cavalry Regiment. Other army units were supposed to meet them at the Little Bighorn River and help them surround the Indians.

Custer had no doubt that he would defeat the Indians. His Seventh Cavalry had already won many victories. As they neared the Little Bighorn, Custer sent out a scouting expedition under Major Marcus Reno. Reno's men were to attack the Indian village from a different direction. But neither Custer nor Reno knew that additional warriors had moved in from outlying areas to join Sitting Bull. More than 2,000 warriors had gathered in and around the camp.

Major Reno's unit got there first and came face-to-face with a huge column of warriors. Reno retreated to the timber and brush along the river, but his men could not hold their position against the larger force. A Lakota chieftain described the scene: "The air was full of smoke and dust. I saw the soldiers fall back and drop into the river bed like buffalo fleeing. . . . The Sioux chased them up the hill." Warriors dashed among the soldiers, hammering them with pistols, rifles, and tomahawks. The warriors killed 40 soldiers and wounded 15 others. Reno led the rest in a hurried flight.

After Reno's retreat, Custer approached the Indian village with his force of 210 men. As they advanced, the warriors surrounded them. Custer's cavalry did not stand a chance. It took less than an hour for the warriors to wipe them out.

Sitting Bull's vision had come true. The Indians had won the Battle of the Little Bighorn. The bloody bodies of Custer and his men lay dead upon the grass. The Indians hurriedly gathered their families and belongings and headed south to the nearby Bighorn Mountains.

News of the massacre at the Little Bighorn spread through the United States. Anger against Native Americans rose even higher. White people labeled Indians a "menace" and demanded their removal once and for all.

THE GHOST DANCERS

The Little Bighorn was the last major victory for the Plains Indians. The United States continued to expand westward. The completion of a coast-to-coast railroad in May 1869 had made traveling faster and easier for western settlers. Towns and cities sprang up along the rail lines. Farms and ranches were established, followed by stores and industries. Silver and gold mines began to appear on western ranges and mountains.

Group after group was forced to settle on reservations. When the reservation land became more valuable—for instance as farmland or when minerals were discovered there—Indians were often moved to a more barren area. "They made us many promises," said one Lakota man, "but they never kept one."

The Indians were filled with despair. So when a Paiute prophet appeared in 1889, many native people were open to his message. His name was Wovoka, and he brought a new religion called the Ghost Dance to Native Americans of the plains region. He said that if Indians danced the rituals of the Ghost Dance, their old ways of life would return: the buffalo would come back; the Indians could live where they wished; and they could ride their horses

Kicking Bear, a Lakota leader of the Ghost Dance religious movement, created this painting of the Battle of the Little Bighorn from memory in 1898. Standing at the left center among the dead, dying, and wounded are *(from left to right)* Chiefs Sitting Bull, Rain-in-the-Face, Crazy Horse, and Kicking Bear.

freely through all their former lands. Wovoka's religion was peaceful. He said the people must not fight or hate. They just had to keep dancing, and their old glory would be restored.

Many white people feared the new religion. They thought it could lead to revolt and violence. They also feared the peaceful dancing. "Indians are dancing in the snow and are wild and crazy," one Indian agent reported to the government in Washington, D.C. He asked for the protection of the army.

By then, Chief Sitting Bull lived with his band on Standing Rock Reservation in South Dakota. He had tried to keep alive the old Indian ways. He had also learned the principles of Wovoka's religion from a Ghost Dance leader. Sitting Bull was an eager student. He was old, but he still had great influence over his people. James McLaughlin, a government agent at the reservation, was afraid that Sitting Bull would unite the Ghost Dancers and lead them in revolt.

On December 15, 1890, McLaughlin sent three Indian policemen to arrest Sitting Bull. As he was being led off, some of his people rushed up to protect their chief. A policeman named Bull Head was shot in the struggle. He turned and fired his pistol into Sitting Bull's chest. A second policeman, Red Tomahawk, shot the chief in the head.

> **EYEWITNESS QUOTE:**
> **ON PRESERVING TRADITION**
>
> "I was born on the prairie where the wind blew free, and there was nothing to break the light of the sun. I lived like my fathers before me....I lived happily. Why do you ask us to leave the rivers, and the sun, and the wind, and to live in houses? Do not ask us to give up the buffalo for the sheep."
>
> —Ten Bears, Comanche chief, 1867

Sitting Bull fell dead. A riot followed. Four policemen and seven followers of Sitting Bull were killed.

After that, wherever the Ghost Dancers gathered, they were set upon and chased off by the army. None of the prophet's claims came true.

THE LAST CAMPAIGN

A few weeks after Sitting Bull's death, in late December, U.S. soldiers caught up with Big Foot and his band of Miniconjou Sioux in South Dakota. There, at Wounded Knee Creek, Big Foot and his band were slaughtered in the last campaign of the Indian wars.

A few weeks later, the army held a great victory parade at Wounded Knee. Regiments marched, and a band played George Armstrong Custer's favorite battle tune. The defeated Lakotas stood on the crest of the hill watching silently.

Occasional raids and skirmishes occurred after the massacre at Wounded Knee, but effective Indian revolts were over. Native Americans had fought thousands of bloody battles for more than 200 years. They had fought bravely to hold on to their lands and freedom. But the U.S. Army was too strong, and the U.S. government was unrelenting in its mission to control the entire continent. By the time of the Wounded Knee massacre, most Indians were living on reservations. The Indian wars had ended.

Indian Schools

Beginning in the late 1800s, the U.S. government took thousands of young Native Americans off their reservations and sent them to white-run boarding schools. In this way, the government hoped to teach young Indians to live as white people did and to break their cultural ties to their own bands, tribes, and nations. Students were made to speak English and were prohibited from using their traditional languages. In many cases, students were not allowed to see their families. Sometimes teachers beat or emotionally abused students.

One of the earliest and most famous Indian school was the Carlisle Indian Industrial School in Pennsylvania. It opened in 1879 under the leadership of U.S. Army brigadier general Richard H. Pratt and remained in operation until 1918. At the Carlisle and other Indian schools, Native American children were taught English, arithmetic, farming, and job skills. Boys studied shoemaking, carpentry, printing, plumbing, and bricklaying, while girls learned sewing, laundering, and cooking. Students were forced to discard their traditional hairstyles and clothing in favor of styles worn by white Americans. But most students who completed their training at these schools were not accepted into white society. Sometimes these Native Americans returned to their reservations to find they were no longer welcome there either.

A few Indian schools offered students a better experience. The Red Cloud Indian School, for instance, was created in 1888 at the Pine Ridge Reservation in South Dakota, home to Oglala Sioux people. The school was created at the request of Native Americans, and Indian leaders were able to watch over its operations. Choctaw and Cherokee people in Oklahoma ran schools that taught young Native Americans to be teachers. Graduates were then able to educate other Native American children.

These Apache students posed for this photograph shortly after their arrival at the Carlisle Indian Industrial School in 1886. School superintendent Richard Pratt is standing back row, center.

EPILOGUE:
THE NEXT CENTURIES

At the end of the 1800s, after two centuries of warfare, disease, and starvation, the Native American population had dwindled from many millions to just 300,000. Strong, proud peoples who had once lived freely along fertile plains and lush woodlands were mostly confined to reservations, where they lived in miserable conditions under the control of the U.S. government. Although they were the original inhabitants of the United States, most Native Americans did not become citizens until 1924, with passage of the Indian Citizenship Act (some Native Americans won their citizenship earlier through

treaties and other procedures). Even after passage of the citizenship act, some states still prohibited Indians from voting.

In 1932 President Franklin Roosevelt appointed John Collier as commissioner of Indian affairs. Collier respected Native American culture and set to work to improve economic conditions on reservations. His efforts resulted in the passage of the Indian Reorganization Act in 1934. This law involved a widespread program for improving Native American life: It gave many Indian tribes and nations the right to adopt their own constitutions and establish governing councils. It ended the

breakup of reservation lands into small parcels, begun by the Dawes Act of 1887. It offered loans to assist Indian governments, farms, and businesses. It improved Native American health care, school systems, and farming programs. The act struck down laws that prohibited Indian religious ceremonies and customs on reservations, and it encouraged Indian artists and the use of native languages.

Just as the Indian Reorganization Act started to improve conditions for Native Americans, World War II (1939–1945) began in Europe. It later spread to Asia and the islands of the Pacific Ocean. The United States entered the war in 1941, and more than 25,000 Native Americans joined the armed forces. In 1942 the Marine Corps recruited Navajo men to create a secret code using the Navajo language. Called code talkers, Navajo speakers sent coded messages over telephones and radios. Their efforts helped the United States win the war.

But after the war, the U.S. government dismantled the programs created by the Indian Reorganization Act. Once more, U.S. leaders tried to get Indians to act more like mainstream white Americans. Government officials argued against isolating Indians on reservations and offering them special loans and assistance.

American Indian Movement leaders Russell Means *(seated, left center)*, Dennis Banks *(seated, right center)*, and other activists sing a victory song after the two men were cleared of wrongdoing at the 1973 Wounded Knee demonstration. AIM continues to fight for Native American rights.

Encouraging self-sufficiency, the government cut funding to Native Americans. It began a program that relocated some Indians from rural reservations into cities. But many Indians had a difficult time adjusting to urban life. In the cities, many suffered from poverty, alcoholism, unemployment, and crime.

In the 1960s, in the wake of the African American civil rights movement, several young Native Americans formed the American Indian Movement (AIM), based in Minneapolis, Minnesota. Many others soon joined. Chapters were set up in 40 cities and reservations. AIM members engaged in marches and sit-ins around the country to protest the discriminatory treatment of their people. One of the most publicized protests took place in 1973 at the historic site of the massacre at Wounded Knee in South Dakota. This demonstration ended in gunfire between protesters and federal agents. Two Indians were killed, but the protest brought the plight of Native Americans to the attention of the public.

Indian activists continued to fight for rights, education, and more control over their own reservations. The government responded with laws and court decisions that restored lands to Native Americans or paid them for lands taken illegally in earlier centuries. The Indian Self-Determination and Education Assistance Act of 1975 gave Indian tribes and nations responsibility for running their own community development, education, health care, housing, and law enforcement programs.

In 1988 Congress passed the Indian Gaming Regulatory Act. This law allowed

Indian tribes and nations to set up gambling casinos on reservations. Although some Native Americans feel that gambling will not, in the long run, solve their economic and social problems, casinos nevertheless provide jobs for Native Americans and profits for Indian nations. The best-known and most successful casino is the Foxwoods in Connecticut, run by the Pequot Nation. The casino's profits are used to provide housing, health care, education, and cultural programs for Pequot people.

Modern Indian life is complex and varied. The Bureau of Indian Affairs lists 562 recognized tribes and nations and approximately 285 reservations. A recent census counted more than two million Native Americans in the United States, about half living on reservations. Indians still struggle with many problems, such as poverty, poor health, and unemployment. They also continue to struggle with the U.S. government over issues such as land and mineral rights.

At the same time, Indians have had many successes in recent years. Many tribes and nations operate casinos and other profitable businesses. Others make money from the sale or lease of oil, natural gas, or minerals on reservation lands. Some Native Americans are active in politics. Others have revived traditional arts, such as weaving, basket making, and pottery. Native rituals, religions, and dances have also undergone a revival in recent years. Native American writers such as Sherman Alexie and Louise Erdrich have won great acclaim for their literary works exploring contemporary Indian life. Movies such as *Smoke Signals* (1998) also offer insight into modern Indian life.

The injustices of the Indians Wars cannot be undone. Nor can modern Native Americans reclaim all their lost lands, languages, and traditions. But modern Native Americans are very proud of their heritage and look to the future with great optimism.

A storyteller shares traditional stories with a group of Native American students. While embracing much of U.S. culture, many Native American peoples are also reclaiming their traditional culture. In this way, Native Americans honor the people and ways of the past and add to the richness of American life.

MAJOR EVENTS OF THE INDIAN WARS

1622	Jamestown
1675–1676	King Philip's War
1689–1697	King William's War
1702–1713	Queen Anne's War
1754–1763	French and Indian War
1763	Chief Pontiac's rebellion and battle at Fort Pontchartrain
1775–1783	American Revolution
1777	Battle of Oriskany
1779	Battle of Minisink
1794	Battle of Fallen Timbers
1803	Louisiana Purchase
1811	Battle of Tippecanoe
1813	Battle of the Thames
1814	Battle of Horseshoe Bend
1817–1818	First Seminole War
1830	Indian Removal Act
1832	Black Hawk War
1835–1842	Second Seminole War
1838–1839	Trail of Tears
1851	Treaty of Fort Laramie
1854	Grattan Massacre
1855–1858	Third Seminole War
1862	Battle of Apache Pass
1864	Long March of the Navajo.
1864	Massacre at Sand Creek
1876	Battle of the Little Bighorn
1890	Massacre at Wounded Knee Creek

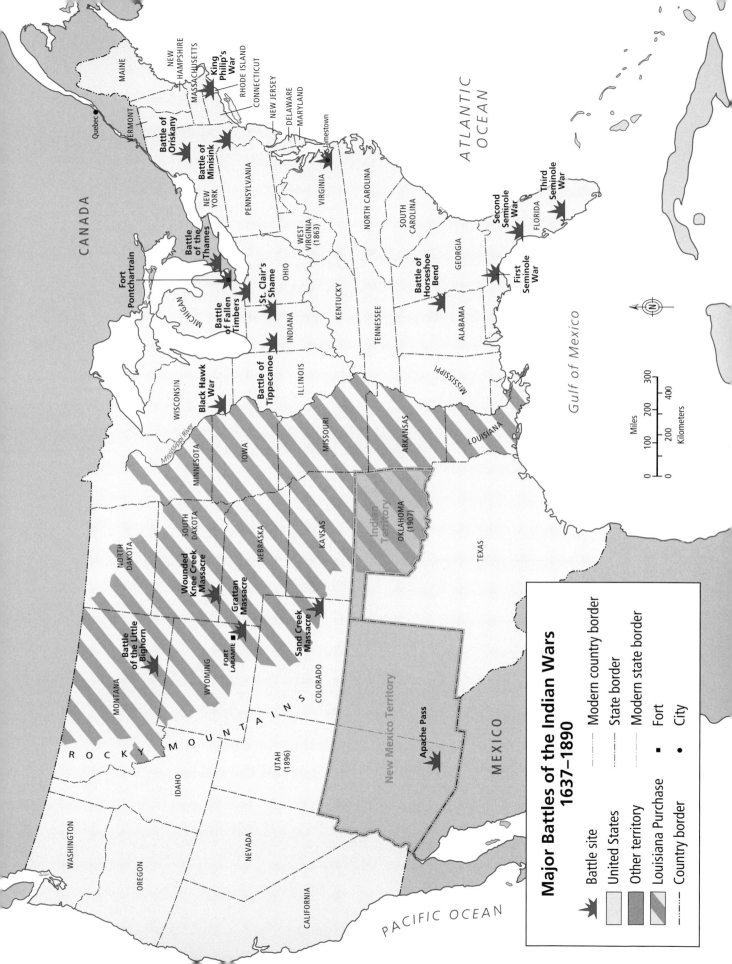

Major Battles of the Indian Wars 1637–1890

CANADA

Quebec

MAINE
NEW HAMPSHIRE
VERMONT
MASSACHUSETTS
King Philip's War
RHODE ISLAND
CONNECTICUT
NEW JERSEY
DELAWARE
MARYLAND

Battle of Oriskany
Battle of Minisink

NEW YORK
PENNSYLVANIA
Jamestown
VIRGINIA
WEST VIRGINIA (1863)
NORTH CAROLINA
SOUTH CAROLINA

ATLANTIC OCEAN

Second Seminole War
Third Seminole War
FLORIDA
First Seminole War

Fort Pontchartrain
Battle of the Thames
Battle of Fallen Timbers
St. Clair's Shame
MICHIGAN
OHIO
KENTUCKY
TENNESSEE
INDIANA
Battle of Tippecanoe
GEORGIA
Battle of Horseshoe Bend
ALABAMA
MISSISSIPPI

Gulf of Mexico

Battle of Fallen Timbers

Black Hawk War

WISCONSIN
Mississippi River
ILLINOIS

MINNESOTA
IOWA
MISSOURI
ARKANSAS
LOUISIANA

Miles
0 100 200 300
Kilometers
0 200 400

Wounded Knee Creek Massacre
Grattan Massacre
Sand Creek Massacre

NORTH DAKOTA
SOUTH DAKOTA
NEBRASKA
KANSAS

Indian Territory
OKLAHOMA (1907)

TEXAS

Battle of the Little Bighorn

FORT LARAMIE
MONTANA
WYOMING
COLORADO

ROCKY MOUNTAINS

New Mexico Territory

Apache Pass

MEXICO

UTAH (1896)
IDAHO
NEVADA
WASHINGTON
OREGON
CALIFORNIA

PACIFIC OCEAN

N

Battle site
United States
Other territory
Louisiana Purchase
Country border

Modern country border
State border
Modern state border
Fort
City

INDIAN WARS TIMELINE

1492	Christopher Columbus makes his first voyage to the New World.
1607	English settlers establish a colony at Jamestown, Virginia.
1620	Pilgrims established Plymouth Colony in Massachusetts.
1622–1644	Powhatan Indians make raids on Jamestown settlers.
1675–1676	King Philip leads several nations against settlers in New England.
1689–1697	French, English, and Indian forces, clash in King William's War.
1702–1713	French, British, and Indian forces fight Queen Anne's War.
1754–1763	French, British, and Indian forces fight the French and Indian War.
1763	Chief Pontiac leads Great Lakes nations against British troops.
1775–1783	American colonists fight for their independence from Great Britain, with different Indian groups allied with the opposing armies.
1777	British, Seneca, and Mohawk forces defeat American colonial troops at the Battle of Oriskany.
1779	Joseph Brant's forces defeat colonial troops at the Battle of Minisink.
1794	Anthony Wayne defeats Little Turtle at the Battle of Fallen Timbers.
1803	The United States buys more than 800,000 square miles of North American territory from France (the Louisiana Purchase).
1811	William Henry Harrison fights Tecumseh's forces at the Battle of Tippecanoe.
1813	Tecumseh is killed by U.S. soldiers at the Battle of the Thames.
1814	Andrew Jackson defeats Creek forces at the Battle of Horseshoe Bend.
1818	Andrew Jackson defeats the Seminole Nation in the First Seminole War.
1830	Congress passes the Indian Removal Act.
1830s	Congress designates parts of Oklahoma as Indian Territory.
1832	U.S. troops defeat Black Hawk's warriors in the Black Hawk War.
1835–1842	Osceola fights U.S. troops in the Second Seminole War.
1838–1839	Winfield Scott's forces march Cherokees to Indian Territory along the so-called Trail of Tears.
1847–1848	White militias fight the Cayuses in Oregon Territory.
1851	Thomas Fitzpatrick signs a treaty with Plains Indian chiefs at Fort Laramie, Wyoming.
1855–1858	Seminoles fight U.S. troops in the Third Seminole War.
1862	U.S. troops clash with Apache warriors at the Battle of Apache Pass.
1862–1864	U.S. troops fight Navahos in the American Southwest.
1864	U.S. troops massacre about 200 Cheyennes at Sand Creek in Colorado.
1876	Sioux and Cheyenne warriors defeat George Custer's Seventh Cavalry at the Battle of the Little Bighorn.
1889	Wovoka spreads the Ghost Dance religion among Plains Indians.
1890	U.S. Cavalry troops massacre Lakota Sioux Indians at Wounded Knee Creek.

GLOSSARY

ambush: a surprise attack, made from a concealed position

animistic religion: a religion based on the belief that spirits reside in natural elements such as wind, water, plants, and animals

cavalry: soldiers who travel into battle on horseback

colony: a settlement in a foreign country with business and political ties to the home country

confederation: an alliance of various groups, states, or nations

homestead: to acquire and settle on public land

Indian Territory: A region in part of Oklahoma, set aside from about 1830 to 1906 as a living place for Indians who had been forcibly relocated by the U.S. government

infantry: soldiers who fight on foot

longhouse: a long, communal dwelling used by the Iroquois and other eastern woodland Indians

manifest destiny: the belief, common in the 1800s, that the United States was destined to control North America from the Atlantic to the Pacific oceans. This belief fueled U.S. government policy of removing Indian people from their historic homelands.

militia: an army made up of citizens instead of professional soldiers

missionaries: religious teachers who try to convert others to their faith

nomads: people who travel from place to place, looking for fresh sources of food and water according to the seasons

reservation: land set aside for and governed by Native Americans

sachem: a Native American chief

shaman: a Native American healer

WHO'S WHO?

Joseph Brant (1742–1807)

A Mohawk warrior, Brant was born in modern-day Ohio. His Mohawk name was Thayendanegea, which means "two sticks tied together for strength." As a child, Brant moved with his mother to New York State. A British agent who worked with the Mohawk sent Joseph to a European-style school in Connecticut. There, the young Mohawks learned Latin, Greek, and English. He then returned to his people and translated the Bible into the Mohawk language. In the 1770s, Brant was made war chief of the six Iroquois nations and raised an army to fight alongside the British during the American Revolution. His army consisted mostly of Mohawks, Cayugas, Senecas, and Onondagas. But some of his soldiers were white men who wore Indian war paint and clothing. They called themselves Brant's Volunteers.

Kit Carson (1809–1868)

Kit Carson was born in Madison County, Kentucky, and raised in the Missouri Territory. He left home at 17 and became a well-known hunter and trapper. He also worked as a scout, guiding expeditions to New Mexico, Colorado, and California. He served with the U.S. Army during the Mexican War, fighting in California. During the Civil War, Carson led infantry volunteers in New Mexico. He later led brutal campaigns against the Indians of the Southwest, subduing the Apaches and the Navajos. Carson was made a brigadier general in 1865.

Crazy Horse (ca. 1844–1877)

Crazy Horse, born near Rapid City, South Dakota, was a member of the Oglala Sioux. As a young man, he fought against U.S. troops under Red Cloud. He married a Cheyenne woman and became chief of a band of Oglalas and Cheyennes who refused to settle on reservations. In 1874 he joined forces with Sitting Bull. In 1876 the two leaders fought U.S. Army forces at the Battle of Rosebud Creek and the Battle of the Little Bighorn. The U.S. Army was determined to capture Crazy Horse and pursued him nonstop. He finally surrendered in Nebraska on May 6, 1877. A few months later, he was killed by a soldier while trying to escape. A monument to Crazy Horse has been carved out of a mountain in the Black Hills of South Dakota. American sculptor Korczak Ziolkowski began the sculpture in the 1940s, and his family is still completing it.

George Armstrong Custer (1839–1876)

George Armstrong Custer was born in New Rumley, Ohio, in 1839. He graduated from West Point, the U.S. Military Academy, in 1861. During the Civil War, his service was so outstanding that he was given command of a cavalry unit and made a brigadier general at the age of 23. After the war, Custer's Seventh Cavalry was sent west to fight Native Americans. In 1876 Lakota and other warriors defeated Custer during the Battle of the Little Bighorn. Custer and all his men were killed in the battle. Custer received a hero's burial at West Point.

Andrew Jackson (1767–1845)

Jackson was born in the Waxhaws region, located on the border of North Carolina and South Carolina. As a young man, Jackson moved to Tennessee, where he became a lawyer. He was elected to the U.S. House of Representatives in 1796 and the U.S. Senate in 1797. In 1802 he became a major general in the Tennessee Militia, and in 1812 he was appointed major general in the U.S. Army. He fought in the War of 1812, the Creek War, and the First Seminole War, earning the nickname Old Hickory for his courage and tough leadership. In 1828 Jackson was elected president of the United States. In this position, he opposed Cherokee land claims in Georgia. He also signed the Indian Removal Act of 1830, which brought about the relocation of the southeastern native peoples to Indian Territory.

Pocahontas (ca. 1595–1617)

Pocahontas, born near Jamestown, Virginia, was the favorite daughter of Chief Powhatan and a great friend to the English settlers at Jamestown. She convinced fellow Indians to save the life of English captain John Smith and later married Englishman John Rolfe. He took her on a visit to England, where she became popular with both the royalty and common people. While still in England, Pocahontas fell ill and died. She and Rolfe had one son, Thomas.

Sacagawea (ca. 1787–1812 or 1884)

Sacagawea was a Shoshone woman who served as a guide and interpreter for the Lewis and Clark Expedition in 1805 and 1806. She had been born in Idaho and captured by an enemy nation. They sold her to a Canadian trapper named Toussaint Charbonneau, and she became his wife. Lewis and Clark hired Charbonneau as a guide in April 1805. Sacagawea went along, carrying her baby son on her back. The expedition members came to depend on Sacagawea. She helped them obtain food and horses and helped them communicate with other Indian peoples. She traveled with the expedition through North Dakota, Montana, Idaho, Washington, and Oregon. She and Charbonneau remained in North Dakota when the expedition returned home. She is believed to have died in 1812. However, an old Native American woman who died on a reservation in 1884 claimed that she was Sacagawea.

Sitting Bull (ca. 1831–1890)

Sitting Bull was one of the last great leaders of Native American resistance in the West. He was born near Grand River in South Dakota in 1831. His Sioux name was Tatanka Iyotake. In 1876 he defeated George Custer's forces at the Battle of the Little Bighorn. Pursued by the U.S. Army, Sitting Bull fled to Canada. U.S. authorities promised to pardon (not punish) Sitting Bull, so he returned to the United States in 1881. The promise was broken. Sitting Bull was imprisoned for two years and then sent to a reservation. Later, Sitting Bull became famous when he toured with Buffalo Bill's Wild West Show—a pageant featuring mock Indian battles and other entertainment. Sitting Bull was shot and killed by a Native American policeman in 1890.

SOURCE NOTES

5 Dee Brown, *Bury My Heart at Wounded Knee* (New York: Holt, Rinehart & Winston, 1970), 444.

5 Ibid., 446.

9 Robert M. Utley and Wilcomb E. Washburn, *The American Heritage History of the Indian Wars* (New York: American Heritage Publishing, 1977), 15.

14 Reader's Digest Association, *Through Indian Eyes: The Untold Story of Native American Peoples* (Pleasantville, NY: Reader's Digest Association, 1995), 130.

14 Daniel K. Richter, *Facing East from Indian Country: A Native History of Early America* (Cambridge, MA: Harvard University Press, 2001), 75.

15 Time-Life Books, *Algonquians of the East Coast* (Alexandria, VA: Time-Life Books, 1993), 89.

17 Alan Taylor, *American Colonies* (New York: Viking, 2001), 395.

19 Utley and Washburn, 86.

19 Ibid., 64.

23 Peter Nabokov, *Native American Testimony: A Chronicle of Indian-White Relations from Prophecy to the Present, 1492–2000,* rev. ed. (New York: Penguin Books, 1999), 93.

24 Ibid., 83.

25 Utley and Washburn, 93.

26 Nabokov, 118.

28 Ibid., 104.

28 Ibid.

28 Ibid., 105.

28 Time-Life Books, *Through Indian Eyes,* 148.

28 Time-Life Books, *Realm of the Iroquois* (Alexandria, VA: Time-Life Books, 1993), 135.

30 Reader's Digest Association, *Through Indian Eyes,* 157.

31 Time-Life Books, *Realm of the Iroquois,* 137.

32 Ibid., 139.

32 Richter, 224.

32 Utley and Washburn, 106.

37 Time-Life Books, *Through Indian Eyes,* 177.

37 Ibid., 179.

38 Ibid., 180.

38 Time-Life Books, *The Mighty Chieftains* (Alexandria, VA: Time-Life Books, 1993), 64.

44 Richter, 235–36.

44 Ibid., 73.

45 Utley and Washburn, 135.

46 Ibid., 137.

47 Time-Life Books, *Through Indian Eyes,* 184.

47 Ibid., 68.

49 Howard Zinn, *A People's History of the United States: 1492–Present,* (New York: HarperCollins, 1999), 101.

51 Time-Life Books, *Through Indian Eyes,* 291.

55 *The West: Indian Reservations.* Spartacus Educational, 2004. <http://www.spartacus.schoolnet.co.uk/WWinreservations.htm> (May 2004).

59 Brown, 199.

59 Ibid., 192.

60 Ibid., 14.

61 Utley and Washburn, 198.

67 Utley and Washburn, 186.

68 Brown, 288.

68 Time-Life Books, *War for the Plains* (Alexandria, VA: Time-Life Books, 1994), 88.

70 Utley and Washburn, 243.

71 Ibid., 294.

72 Ibid., 295.

72 Time-Life Books, *The Mighty Chieftains,* 163.

SELECTED BIBLIOGRAPHY, FURTHER READING, & WEBSITES

SELECTED BIBLIOGRAPHY

Algonquians of the East Coast. Alexandria, VA: Time-Life Books, 1993.

Anderson, Fred. *Crucible of War.* New York: Vintage Books, 2000.

Axelrod, Alan. *Chronicle of the Indian Wars.* New York: Prentice Hall, 1993.

Brown, Dee. *Bury My Heart at Wounded Knee.* New York: Holt, Rinehart & Winston, 1970.

The Buffalo Hunters. Alexandria, VA: Time-Life Books, 1993.

Carlson, Paul H. *The Plains Indians.* College Station: Texas A&M University Press, 1998.

Grant, Bruce. *Encyclopedia of the American Indian.* New York: Wing Books, 1989.

McCartney, Laton. *Across the Great Divide.* New York: The Free Press, 2003.

The Mighty Chieftains. Alexandria, VA: Time-Life Books, 1993.

Nabokov, Peter. *Native American Testimony: A Chronicle of Indian-White Relations from Prophecy to the Present, 1492–2000.* Rev. ed. New York: Penguin Books, 1999.

Realm of the Iroquois. Alexandria, VA: Time-Life Books, 1993.

The Reservations. Alexandria, VA: Time-Life Books, 1995.

Richter, Daniel K. *Facing East from Indian Country: A Native History of Early America.* Cambridge, MA: Harvard University Press, 2001.

Robinson, Charles M., III. *A Good Year to Die.* New York: Random House, 1995.

Sugden, John. *Tecumseh: A Life.* New York: Henry Holt & Co., 1997.

Taylor, Alan. *American Colonies.* New York: Viking, 2001.

Through Indian Eyes: The Untold Story of Native American Peoples. Pleasantville, NY: Reader's Digest Association, 1995.

Utley, Robert M., and Wilcomb E. Washburn. *The American Heritage History of the Indian Wars.* New York: American Heritage Publishing, 1977.

Viola, Herman J. *North American Indians.* New York: Crown, 1996.

War for the Plains. Alexandria, VA: Time-Life Books, 1994.

The Way of the Warrior. Alexandria, VA: Time-Life Books, 1993.

Zinn, Howard. *A People's History of the United States: 1492–Present.* New York: HarperCollins, 1999.

FURTHER READING

Aleshire, Peter. *The Apache Wars.* New York: Facts on File, 1998.

Behrman, Carol H. *Andrew Jackson.* Minneapolis: Lerner Publications Company, 2003.

Bohannon, Lisa Fredrickson. *The American Revolution.* Minneapolis, Lerner Publications Company, 2005.

Cheatham, Kae. *Dennis Banks: Native American Activist.* Springfield, NJ: Enslow, 1997.

Childress, Diana. *The War of 1812.* Minneapolis: Lerner Publications Company, 2004.

Cunningham, Chet. *Chief Crazy Horse.* Minneapolis: Lerner Publications Company, 2000.

Erlich, Amy, and Dee Alexander Brown. *Wounded Knee: An Indian History of the American West.* New York: Henry Holt, 1993.

Feldman, Ruth Tenzer. *The Mexican-American War.* Minneapolis: Lerner Publications Company, 2004.

Hoag, Stanley. *Night of the Cruel Moon.* New York: Facts on File, 1996.

Kent, Zachary. *General Armstrong Custer: Civil War General and Western Legend.* Springfield, NJ: Enslow, 2000.

Sneve, Virginia Driving Hawk. *The Apaches.* New York: Holiday House, 1997.

Stefoff, Rebecca. *Tecumseh and the Shawnee Confederation.* New York: Facts on File, 1998.

WEBSITES

National Museum of the American Indian. This site offers extensive information about Native American culture.
<http://www.nmai.si.edu>

Nativeculture.com. This site serves as a portal to other Native American materials on the Internet. It has links to American Indian Radio, books for young readers, the American Indian Library Association, native nations, and more.
<http://www.nativeculture.com>

New Perspectives on the West. This site, a companion to the PBS miniseries *The West,* examines the history of the American West, Native Americans, and the Indian wars from the 1500s to 1917.
<http://www.pbs.org/weta/thewest/>

INDEX

ABOUT THE AUTHOR

Carol H. Behrman was born in Brooklyn, New York. She graduated from City College of New York and attended Columbia University's Teachers' College, where she majored in education. She married Edward Behrman, an accountant, and moved to Fair Lawn, New Jersey, where they raised three children. They currently reside in Sarasota, Florida.

For many years, Behrman taught grades five through eight at the Glen Ridge Middle School in New Jersey. She has written twenty-three books, fiction and nonfiction, for children and young adults, as well as seven writing textbooks.

PHOTO ACKNOWLEDGMENTS

The images in this book are used with the permission of: © Bettmann/CORBIS, pp. 4–5, 38, 76; Confederation Life Gallery of Canadian History, p. 6; © The British Museum, p. 7; Lois E. Clark, p. 8; Laura Westlund (maps), pp. 11, 18, 29, 35, 41, 52, 64, 78; #3376004, Harold R. Walters/American Museum of Natural History, p. 12; Jacques Francis Lee, Minnesota Historical Society Art Collection, p. 16; National Archives of Canada, p. 17 (c1026); courtesy of the Library of Congress/John J. McDonough and Janice E. Ruth, Manuscript Division, p. 21; © North Wind Picture Archives, pp. 22, 24, 26, 43; Harold C. Furlong/New York State Museum of Science and Service, p. 25; Library of Congress, pp. 28 (LC-USZ62-45198), 33 (LC-USZ62-52050), 59 (left) (LC-USZC4-5661), 59 (right) (LC-USZC4-8838), 62 (LC-USZ62-107576), 65 (Journal of the Senate of the United States, Volume 43), 68 (LC-USZ62-111147), 69 (LC-USZC4-6161), 82 (bottom) (LC-USZ62-22437), 83 (bottom) (LC-USZ62-111147); Metropolitan Toronto Reference Library, J. Ross Robertson Collection (MTL 2013), pp. 31, 82 (top); "The Trail of Tears" by Robert Lindneux, from the original oil painting in Woolaroe Museum, Bartlesville, OK, p. 40; General Research Division, New York Public Library, p. 42; © "Osceola, the Black Drink, Distinguished Warrior" by George Catlin, National Collection of Fine Arts, Smithsonian American Art Museum, Washington, D.C./Art Resource, NY, p. 44; American Antiquarian Society, p. 45; Wisconsin Historical Society (WHi-21522), p. 46; © Hulton| Archive by Getty Images, pp. 50, 83 (second from top, second from bottom); Montana Historical Society, Haynes Foundation Collection, p. 53; National Archives, pp. 54 (War and Conflict Collection), 63 (top) (NWDNS-79-M-1B-3); © The Charles Parker Gallery, p. 56; © Smithsonian American Art Museum, Washington, D.C./Art Resource, NY, p. 57; © Smithsonian Institution National Anthropological Archives, Bureau of American Ethnology Collection, p. 60; Montana State University—Billings, p. 63 (bottom); #326847, Short Bull/American Museum of Natural History, p. 70; courtesy of Southwest Museum, Los Angeles, p. 71; U.S. Army Military History Research Collection, Carlisle Barracks, PA, p. 73; © Smithsonian Institution, pp. 75–75 (56,630); © Bob Rowan/Progressive Image/CORBIS, p. 77; Starsmore Center for Local History, Colorado Springs Pioneers Museum, p. 82 (center); © Eastern National/courtesy of the Horseshoe Bend National Military Park, p. 83 (top).

Cover: The Denver Pubic Library, Western History Collection, X-31486.